T0286948

Cambridge Elements ≡

Elements in Public and Nonprofit Administration
edited by
Andrew Whitford
University of Georgia
Robert Christensen
Brigham Young University

COOPETITION

How Interorganizational Collaboration Shapes Hospital Innovation in Competitive Environments

Ling Zhu
University of Houston

CAMBRIDGE
UNIVERSITY PRESS

University Printing House, Cambridge CB2 8BS, United Kingdom

One Liberty Plaza, 20th Floor, New York, NY 10006, USA

477 Williamstown Road, Port Melbourne, VIC 3207, Australia

314–321, 3rd Floor, Plot 3, Splendor Forum, Jasola District Centre,
New Delhi – 110025, India

79 Anson Road, #06–04/06, Singapore 079906

Cambridge University Press is part of the University of Cambridge.

It furthers the University's mission by disseminating knowledge in the pursuit of education, learning, and research at the highest international levels of excellence.

www.cambridge.org
Information on this title: www.cambridge.org/9781108963985
DOI: 10.1017/9781108966634

© Ling Zhu 2021

This publication is in copyright. Subject to statutory exception and to the provisions of relevant collective licensing agreements, no reproduction of any part may take place without the written permission of Cambridge University Press.

First published 2021

A catalogue record for this publication is available from the British Library.

ISBN 978-1-108-96398-5 Paperback
ISSN 2515-4303 (online)
ISSN 2515-429X (print)

Cambridge University Press has no responsibility for the persistence or accuracy of URLs for external or third-party internet websites referred to in this publication and does not guarantee that any content on such websites is, or will remain, accurate or appropriate.

Coopetition

How Interorganizational Collaboration Shapes Hospital Innovation in Competitive Environments

Elements in Public and Nonprofit Administration

DOI: 10.1017/9781108966634
First published online: May 2021

Ling Zhu
University of Houston

Author for correspondence: Ling Zhu, lzhu4@central.uh.edu

Abstract: Public service innovation, defined as the adoption of new technology and methods of service delivery, is at the heart of public management research. Scholars have long studied public and private sector innovation as distinctive phenomena, arguing that private sector innovation aims to increase firms' competitive advantage, while public sector innovation purports to improve governance and performance. The public–private dichotomy overlooks the complex way in which organizations interact with one another for service delivery. Public services are increasingly delivered through the web of collaborative networks, in which organizations compete and cooperate simultaneously. This Element explores how coopetition, namely the simultaneous presence of competition and collaboration, shapes innovation in the health care sector. Analyzing panel data of 4,000+ American hospitals from 2008 to 2017, this Element finds evidence that coopetition catalyzes the technology and service process innovation and offers practical implications on managing innovation in competitive environments.

Keywords: innovation, coopetition, competition, collaboration, hospitals, health care

© Ling Zhu 2021

ISBNs: 9781108963985 (PB), 9781108966634 (OC)
ISSNs: 2515-4303 (online), 2515-429X (print)

Contents

1 Introduction: Interorganizational Dynamics and Innovation

Public service innovation, namely, the adoption of new ideas, technology, and methods of public service delivery (Vries, Bekkers, and Tummers, 2018; Walker, 2008), is of growing importance for governments and frontline public service organizations. Diverse societies and the rapidly changing "policyscape" produce challenges to policy maintenance and effective implementation (Mettler, 2016). Evolving societal, political, and technological factors and changing demands on various public services drive service organizations to make innovative adaptations to their external market and political environment (Leyden and Link, 2015).

Conventionally, scholars have studied public and private sector innovation as distinctive phenomena, arguing that private sector innovation primarily aims to increase firms' survivability and their profit margins, while public sector innovation is to achieve improvements in governance and performance (Moore, 1995). Since the 1990s, many public sector organizations have adopted pro-competition reforms and technology innovation to improve the efficiency and effectiveness of public service delivery, making innovation a central theme in public management and public policy research (Osborne and Brown, 2005). Following the diffusion of New Public Management (NPM), there has been an outpouring of empirical studies that focus on different types of innovation at both the individual and the organizational level, such as process reform, technology innovation, product or service innovation, and knowledge creation (Vries, Bekkers, and Tummers, 2018; Yao and Walker, 2019).

In spite of the different goals and types of innovation seen in the public and private sectors, theories and empirical studies regarding why organizations change and innovate abound. Four approaches of studying organizational innovation emerge from the existing literature: (1) theories of rational firms and innovation focus on market competition and organizational capacity as the main drivers of innovation; (2) the literature on innovation management gives particular attention to leadership priority and leadership style; (3) resource dependency theory considers an organization's political, social, and economic environment as drivers of innovation; and (4) theories of interorganizational networks deem collaborative relationships as the main venue for learning and the diffusion of innovation.

Scholars of rational firms conceptualize organizational behavior such as innovation and organizational change as the result of "learning from the market" (Bouwen and Fry, 1991; Levitt and March, 1988; Salge, 2011; Teece, 1992). Decisions of adopting innovation, in this literature, are thought to be routine-based and goal-oriented bounded rational behavior. Under this premise, scholars in this camp have advanced knowledge regarding how the need for innovation and change stem from organizations' rational assessment of goal achievement (performance) (e.g., Nicholson et al., 2017; Salge, 2011; Zhu and Rutherford, 2019), resource slacks, and organizational competence. For example, organizational size, entrepreneurship, and available high-skill human capital (Kimberly and Evanisko, 1981) are recognized as major internal drivers of innovation. Following the same premise of the bounded-rationality model, numerous studies also examined how external market competition drives innovation outputs and firm investment in research and development (R&D) (Aghion et al., 2005; Negassi and Hung, 2014). The emphasis on the internal antecedents of innovation has also been the subject of empirical examination regarding public sector innovation. Walker (2014) surveys the literature on local government innovation and concludes that organizational size, administrative capacity, and organizational learning are key drivers of local government innovation. These internal antecedents are rarely studied in relation to external determinants in the literature. Analyzing the English National Health Service (NHS) System, Salge (2011) concludes innovation decisions in British hospitals follow the rational behavioral model, which is defined by the slack search process (excessive resources) and problem search process (negative performance feedback).

In a different camp, scholars of innovation management conceptualize innovation as an organizational output shaped by entrepreneurship (Windrum and Koch, 2008), leadership quality (Lewis et al., 2018), leadership style (Hughs et al., 2018; Jung, Wu, and Chow, 2008; Martin, Currie, and Finn, 2009), and top-level managerial priorities (Damanpour and Schneider, 2006). The leadership approach of innovation research focuses on top leaders as the human agents of change. Empirical evidence on how leaders matter for organizational innovation converges between studies on private sector firms and public sector organizations. For example, Jung, Wu, and Chow (2008) find a positive relationship between CEO transformational leadership and firms' innovativeness. Similar evidence is reported in the Lewis et al. (2018) study in public sector innovation.

The third theoretical approach of organizational innovation focuses on the external contingencies of organizations. The external contingency approach of innovation centers on the idea that organizations are dependent on their external political, social, and economic environment for resources, stakeholder support, and reputation. This approach is a core extension of the open system theory. (Katz and Kahn, 1978; Pfeffer and Salancik, 1978). In their seminal book, The *External Control of Organizations*, Pfeffer and Salancik (1978) highlight the notion that, for organizational choices and decisions to be understood, it is necessary to focus on the external social context rather than internal factors and leaders' values and beliefs. In a nutshell, the external contingency perspective recognizes that organizations engage in innovation activities in accordance with their assessment of various external resource constraints and different client inputs (Aldrich and Ruff, 2006; DiMaggio and Powell, 1983; Pfeffer and Salancik, 1978).

The idea that embedded social relationships can spark change has later been further developed by organizational scholars who are interested in interfirm social networks (e.g., Uzzi, 1997), and policy scholars who are puzzled about the adoption and diffusion of policy innovations in the government sector. In this literature, scholars focus primarily on how policy networks, socially embedded relationships, and collaborative interactions produce policy innovation (Balla, 2001; Bennett and Howlett, 1992; Howlett and Koppenjan, 2017; Nicholson-Crotty, 2009). Similar to the external contingency perspective, scholars of interorganizational collaboration emphasize the role of the external social environment in driving organizational behavior. The network of interdependencies and social relationships form channels of learning, knowledge diffusion, and isomorphic pressures for change and innovation (DiMaggio and Powell, 1983; Powell, 1990; Powell and DiMaggio, 1991). Social embeddedness and organizational networks, according to Uzzi (1997), also enable organizations to make complex adaptations and reach collective problem-solving arrangements, thus facilitating innovation.

The existing literature provides diverse theoretical approaches to examining the key drivers of innovation, with increasing attention to the horizontal interorganizational relationships and innovation (Provan, Fish, and Sydow, 2007). However, most previous studies overlook the complex way in which organizations interact with each other and examine interorganizational competition and collaboration as two opposite ends on a single continuum, as distinctive drivers of change and innovation. In fact, the line between public and private service sector service production is blurred, as many public services are increasingly delivered through interorganizational networks that connect organizations from both the public and private sectors, which may produce complex interorganizational dynamics. On the one hand, service organizations may collaborate with one another because of shared goals and complementary resources and expertise. On the other hand, service organizations may coexist in the same local market and compete with one another for clients, funding, and human capital. How do such complex interorganizational dynamics, namely, collaboration and competition, affect innovation?

To advance knowledge on how complex interorganizational dynamics affect innovation, I integrate literatures on interorganizational collaboration, market competition, and theories of coopetition. The theoretical framework of this research draws from the external contingency perspective, by focusing on how external interorganizational relationships affect innovation activities. It centers on the concept of coopetition (Brandenburger and Nalebuff, 1996), which conceptualizes competition and collaboration as two connected interorganizational dynamics that drive various innovation activities (Bunger et al., 2020; Devece et al., 2019; Hartley et al., 2013; Lado et al., 1997). Focusing on the simultaneous presence of competition and collaboration across organizations, the theoretical framework connects with the external contingency perspective of innovation by focusing on interorganizational interactions rather than internal organizational factors.

Specifically, I argue that market competition and interorganizational collaboration are two different yet interconnected forces that drive innovation under different mechanisms (Lado et al., 1997; Tsai, 2002). Competition exists among organizations that produce mutually substitutable services, serve the similar client populations, and are dependent on the same labor-force pool (Bunger et al. 2020). Collaboration is driven by shared interests, common external challenges, and stakeholder preferences. Following Lado et al. (1997), I conceptualize four different scenarios of horizontal interorganizational relationships: *isolated monopoly, neck-to-neck competition between silo organizations, highly networked world*, and *coopetition*. An isolated monopoly emerges when an organization does not have any competitor and does not collaborate with others. Neck-to-neck competition between silo organizations occurs when organizations engage with one another only by competitive relationships and form no collaborative ties. In the highly networked world, collaboration is high and competition among partners is low. Coopetition arises when dense collaborative relationships exist in highly competitive markets.

Using this typology, I explore how the interplay between competition and collaboration drives the adoption of various innovations. Competitive pressures from local service markets drive innovation, particularly the adoption of low-cost service innovation, because intense competition motivates organizations to put an emphasis on innovation activities that will help them to expand revenue sources and clients (Aghion, Howitt, and Prantl, 2013). Innovation, nevertheless, can be costly to organizations, such as the adoption of new technology that requires a large amount of initial investment. Intensive competition thus might turn organizations into a less innovative mode and increase the favorability of the status quo. In such situations, collaborative networks can help organizations retain costs associated with innovation in various ways. First, collaborative networks facilitate innovation by reducing both the cost and uncertainty of innovation. Second, collaborative networks are channels for diffusing new knowledge and information. Thus, in competitive markets, high-cost technology innovation can increase through collaborative channels (Ritala and Sainio, 2013).

The American health care sector, whereby innovation is key to improve service quality, offers an ideal empirical context to examine the links between the interorganizational dynamics of coopetition. In the USA, health care provider organizations (hospitals) in all three sectors are responsible for delivering health care to patients. Hospitals from different sectors produce and deliver health care services based on comparable medical industry standards. Hospitals from the same area often engage in interorganizational collaborations for more effective service delivery. Meanwhile, hospitals in the same local area compete with one another for government funding, patients (especially Medicare patients), health care professionals, and are often engaging in competitive bidding for health insurance contracts (Keijser and Kirkman-Liff, 1992). The complex interorganizational dynamics make it possible to examine how collaborative and competition jointly affect innovation in the health care sector.

The empirical analysis is based on a panel study of 4,000+ American hospitals from 2008 to 2017, an empirical sample covering about 75 percent of the American hospitals from the public, nonprofit, and private sectors. The longitudinal panel dataset covers years before and after the enactment of the Affordable Care Act (ACA) 2010 that introduced substantial changes to hospitals' local health care markets and accountability requirements on cost containment and performance management. Salient changes in national- and subnational-level health policies under the ACA create opportunities and incentives for hospital innovation and variations in the pace of innovation across the three sectors and hospital locations. Using dynamic panel data models, I analyze innovation in several thousands of hospitals based on multiple innovation indicators: hospitals' adoption of new medical technology, such as robotic surgery and electronic health records, the adoption of mobile health care and telemedicine, and pioneering hospitals that adopted patient-centered care models, such as the Patient-Centered Medical Home Program (PCMH) and the Accountable Care Organization (ACO). I find robust evidence that coopetition significantly affects the adoption of innovation, albeit that the links between coopetition and innovation vary by innovation areas. For technology innovation with spiraling costs, coopetition accelerates the adoption. Hospitals that simultaneously have a high level of market competition and collaborative service delivery are most likely to pursue expensive new medical technology. For patient-oriented service innovation, strong inter-hospital collaboration and low-competitive pressures are associated with a greater likelihood of adoption. Regardless of the specific innovation type, nevertheless, isolated monopolies are found to be the laggards of innovation in most cases.

This research makes several contributions. First, this research generalizes the link between interorganizational collaboration and innovation across all three sectors, thus it differs from prior studies that focus on service innovation just in one sector. This research also speaks to the rich literature that links organizational innovation to the external environment (Akkerman and Torenvlied, 2011, Boyne and Meier, 2009; Meier and O'Toole, 2015), by highlighting that both interorganizational collaboration and competition offer new ways of thinking about service organizations' social-environmental contexts. Third, this research adds to the literature on the sociology of institutions (Powell, 1990) by showing the interactive effects of interorganizational collaboration and market competition. Demonstrating that organizations are embedded within market structures and collaborative relationships, the coopetition framework broadens the understanding of service innovation in more complex interorganizational contexts. As the existing literature on coopetition and innovation largely remains to be small-N qualitative and primarily focuses on business firms (McCarthy et al., 2018) moreover, there is only suggestive evidence that coopetition between organizations better motivates innovation than competitive pressures simply coming from the market (LeTourneau, 2004; Yami and Nemeh, 2014). This research fills in the gap by providing a large-N systematic analysis of how interorganizational collaboration in competitive environments shapes innovation. Different from studies that focus on a small number of networks and take the whole-network approach (Bunger et al., 2020), the empirical analysis traces a nationally representative sample of hospitals in a ten-year period. Key empirical findings shed light on practical strategies for promoting service innovation. While organizations might be constrained by great competitive pressures, forming and managing collaborative relationships with peer organizations can help to buffer the negative impact of pernicious competition.

Section 2 lays out the theoretical framework of coopetition. Discussion on key expectations follows, showing how innovation varies along with interorganizational competition and collaboration. Sections 3 to 5 focus on empirically exploring the joint effects of competition and collaboration on the adoption of different forms of health care innovation, including the adoption of high-cost new medical technology, relatively low-cost service innovation that improves the accessibility of service, and patient-centered payment innovation incentivized by the ACA. Section 6 summarizes key findings, makes recommendations for future research on interorganizational dynamics, and concludes with practical implications on how to manage innovation in competitive environments.

2 The Theoretical Framework of Coopetition

Being at the forefront of effective policymaking and public service delivery, frontline service organizations produce and deliver social services to citizens in a wide range of policy domains, such as education, welfare, health, and human services. These organizations also translate numerous federal and state government grants into service innovation activities that directly affect policy outcomes and citizens' wellbeing (de Lancer Julnes and Gibson, 2016; Hicklin and Godwin, 2009).

The general topic of organizational behavior in innovation adoption has been an expansive research area in both the public and private management literature (Kimberley and Evanisko, 1981). There is a large literature embracing the theme that large service organizations, especially those in the public sector, are inertial. Pressman and Wildavsk's (1984) classic book on local implementation of federal policies shows the difficulty of bringing change to the frontline (Weick, 1979). Research and development (R&D) produce new policy ideas and technology innovations, which do not automatically transfer from laboratories of innovation to the field of implementation (Bozeman, 2000). Recent studies that focus on the frontline innovation adoption show a mixed picture about the fate of new ideas and technology in the public service sector (Maroulis, 2009). Reactive management strategies, in addition, also impede innovation. Some leaders of public organizations and nonprofit managers either react to policy reforms passively or try their best to buffer external environmental turbulence (Lynn, 2005; Meier and O'Toole, 2008; Weick and Sutcliffe, 2007). As leaders in these organizations often face the paradox of organizing and innovating, they could develop a risk-aversion mindset and to change (Kelman, 2005).

In spite of the barriers to change, scholars do find various innovation activities in a wide range of public service domains. There is a long-established view that organizations evolve and accept new ideas and technology according to changes in their external environment (Aldrich and Ruff, 2006). Leaders of service organizations can strategically manage the external environment (Akkerman and Torenvlied, 2011; Meier and O'Toole, 2001) and advocate public values (Johansen and LeRoux, 2013) through networking activities with external stakeholders and forming collaborative partnerships with peer organizations. These collaborative relationships thus can become the locus of innovation (Perry-Smith and Mannucci, 1997; Powell, Koput, and Smith-Doerr, 1996). As Perry-Smith and Mannucci (1997: 53) summarize, social networks and networking relationships have been increasingly used as a theoretical lens to study the conception of new ideas (knowledge creation) and the implementation of new ideas (innovation adoption) (Baer, 2010; Burt, 2004; Uzzi and Spiro, 2005).

Much less is known, however, about how interorganizational collaboration and the external market environment may interactively affect service organizations' innovation. In the following subsection, I use the framework of coopetition to explore how horizontal relationships between organizations can be conceptualized based on the two distinct, yet interconnected dimensions: competition and collaboration. Of interest in this research is the adoption of innovation as organizational behavior, and how such innovation activity is linked to horizontal interorganizational relationships.

2.1 Coopetition: The Typology for Conceptualizing Horizontal Interorganizational Relationships

The practice of coopetition is far from being new in the business world. The volatile and uncertain market environment makes strategic alliances and collaboration with business competitors a widespread phenomenon in the private sector (Ritala, Golnam, and Wegmann, 2014). Devece et al. (2019) provide one of the most recent systematic literature reviews on coopetition in the private sector management literature. They point out that coopetition is particularly prevalent among small and medium-sized enterprises (SMEs), because they often coexist with other enterprises in a crowded marketplace, inherently weak in organizational capacity, and often face external constraints on revenue. Because of the widespread practice of coopetition among firms, this concept was first studied by business management scholars. It is widely accepted that Brandenburger and Nalebuff (1996) are the first authors who formalized the concept of coopetition in their game-theory model and case studies of firm strategies for survival and success. At its inception, the term is defined as collaboration with competitors (Devece et al., 2019), and has later been generalized to describe complex horizontal interorganizational relationships based on the interlock of cooperation and competition.

More recently, scholars in public management and nonprofit management began to find the concept of coopetition applicable to a variety of public and nonprofit service organizations, especially in areas such as education, health, and social services. Although direct competition for profit or operating margins is rare, public and nonprofit service organizations are facing increasing interorganizational competition for clients, specialized human capital, government funding, and private donors (Hu, Huang, and Chen, 2019; Moczulksa et al., 2019). Just as SMEs in the business world, public and nonprofit service organizations are often small and medium in size, face resource constraints, and need to compete for survival in their local service areas. In a recent study in a homeless service delivery network, Hu, Huang, and Chen (2019) find that although networked service providers collaborate on service delivery, they *compete* for scarce resources such as government grants and private donations.

In many human and health service areas, public and nonprofit organizations also face cross-sector competition as private for-profits penetrate the local service market (Amirkhanyan, 2008). For example, in his analysis of nonprofit health care organizations, Tuckman (1998) finds that, in nonprofit marketplaces, nonprofit organizations not only compete with one another, but also compete with for-profit providers. Rivalry pressure from mixed markets has led to the commercialization of nonprofits. Meanwhile, many public and nonprofit service organizations are inherently knowledge intensive. The need for effective knowledge sharing in delivering services make collaborative episodes common in public and nonprofit sectors (Willem and Buelens, 2007). In health care and social service sectors, coopetition has gained increasing attention and been explored at the interorganizational level between different provider organizations (Gee, 2000; LeTourneau, 2004) and at the whole-network level (Peng and Bourne, 2009).

The competition perspective focuses on competitive relationships across organizations and recognizes the "invisible hands" of the market as a key feature of the external environment to organizations. The collaborative perspective, by contrast, emphasizes interdependence as the defining feature of the external environment. Neither approach, however, sufficiently describes the complex horizontal interorganizational relationships seen in the process of public service delivery. As Lado et al. (1997: 111) contend, a "syncretic model of competition and cooperation" is needed, and "some synergies of scholarship may be realized from the dynamic interplay between concepts of competition and cooperation." In their study of rent-seeking behavior, Lado et al. (1997) develop a two-by-two typology of different rent-seeking behavior based on the dimensions of interorganizational competition and cooperation. Lado's typology of rent-seeking behavior is well-suited to be generalizable to describe the four types of interorganizational relationship jointly defined by competition and collaboration. Figure 1 applies the Lado et al. (1997) typology to depict varying forms of interorganizational interactions. The same conceptualization also can be found in Stentoft, Mikkelsen, and Ingstrup's (2018) recent discussion on the "coopetition segments" model. In a nutshell, this typology framework classifies interorganizational relationships into four scenarios, depending on the interplay between competition and collaboration.

The first scenario is labeled as *isolated monopoly*, whereby an organization is a sole provider of certain public services in its local area, facing no

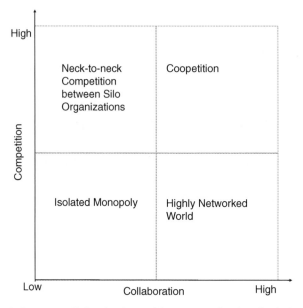

Figure 1 Conceptualizing horizontal inter-organizational relationships: competition, collaboration, and coopetition

competition from other service providers and having no collaborative part-ners. Isolated monopoly is not uncommon in public service delivery. In the American health care sector, for example, many rural hospitals serve as the sole provider of hospital care in their market area (Holmes et al., 2006). Isolated monopoly can occur not only based on geographic locations, but also can emerge due to the specific clients it serves. For example, health care providers in the USA often crowd in urban areas with high population density. Urban public safety hospitals could be monopolist providers to the low-income population and/or uninsured population. Veteran Affairs (VA) medical facilities represent another kind of monopoly – they exclusively serve the veteran population.

Interorganizational interactions increase as the number of service providers increases in the same area or for the same client population. Depending on the level of competition and collaboration, there could be three different scenarios: *highly networked world, neck-to-neck competition*, and *coopetition*. Highly net-worked world refers to strong reciprocal and collaborative relationships between organizations with very little tension of mutual competition. In this setting, collective interests and networking activities prevail. Guo and Acar (2005) recognize the prominent role of nonprofit organizations in urban public service delivery. They also demonstrate interorganizational collaboration, in its varying forms, is prevalent among nonprofits across a wide range of service sectors, including human service, education, health, arts, culture, and humanities. In the absence of interdependence and collaboration, when a local service area crowds with service organizations that are mutually substitutable, they would engage with neck-to-neck competition. In this scenario, rivalry pressure is high, and the intense competition often results in zero-sum games of resource allocation.

The coopetition scenario refers to the interorganizational interactions that comprised of competition and collaboration, for instance, the presence of a crowded and competitive market in the web of socially embedded relationships (DiMaggio and Powell, 1983). Lado et al. (1997) describe the coopetition scenario as syncretic competition, which is different from the zero-sum neck-to-neck competition. Zero-sum competition rises from mutual substitution in the market rivalry. Coopetition refers to rivalry in the end-product/service and core resource areas, but collaboration in knowledge creation, knowledge transfer, and problem-solving (Ritala and Hurmelinna-Laukkanen, 2009). For example, in business and nonprofit sectors, tensions from interorganizational competition are often mitigated by organizational leaders' professional and personal ties (Hu, Huang, and Chen, 2019; Hughes and Goldenhar, 2012; Ibarra and Hunter, 2007).

The presence of collaborative relationships will turn market rivalry into a positive-sum game and alter the key motivation of innovation in competitive markets. In the zero-sum game of market competition, the goal of competition is to maximize profit margins by eliminating competitors and increase market share growth. In the coopetition scenario, the goal of competition is to eliminate the "the-winner-takes-all" dynamics and to increase the total size of the market and collective benefits. The competitive process in the collaborative context will lead to "knowledge and economic, technical, and market growth" (Lado et al., 1997: 122), producing a positive-sum game. In this scenario, interorganizational dynamics are characterized by joint resource and information consumption, intensive communication and other types of networking activity, and complexity due to the potential tension between competition and interdependence (Stetfof, Kikkelsen, and Ingstrup, 2018).

2.2 Networking, Collaboration, and Innovation

How does the interplay between competition and collaboration shape public service innovation? The typology of interorganizational relationships in Figure 1 provides a succinct starting point from which to explore and compare innovation activities under the four different scenarios. In this subsection, I focus on comparing innovation when a public service organization is an isolated monopoly versus when a service area is a highly networked world, filled with networking and collaboration activities.

Since the 1990s, the concept of interorganizational collaboration has received renewed interest among public management and public policy scholars. Connecting insights from social network analysis (Milward and Provan,1998) and collaborative governance (Ansell and Gash, 2008), scholars have advanced this research area by studying the formation and consequences of collaborative relationships (Berry et al., 2004; Isett et al., 2011; Robinson, 2006). While some scholars take a whole-network approach by tracing the evolving structure and institutional characteristics of policy networks (Berardo, 2009; Huang, 2014; Milward and Provan,1998), others take an egocentric approach by focusing on institutional actors (i.e., organizations) and the collaborative relationships between them (DiMaggio and Powell, 1983; Feiock, 2013; Galaskiewicz, 1985; Klijn, 1996).

Research on interorganizational collaboration has proliferated and focused on how interdependent relationships, such as networks and collaborative part-nerships, affect organizational behavior and success (Gazley, 2017). One major theme of this literature highlights the role of interorganizational collaboration in facilitating innovation, especially innovation in human service organizations and knowledge-intensive service areas. This literature suggests four different mechanisms through which interorganizational collaboration can promote innovation: (1) innovation of capacity building through scaling up resources, (2) mitigating risk and building external stakeholder support for change, (3) facilitating knowledge creation and speeding up knowledge diffusion, and (4) spreading the norm of innovation within networks.

First, networks of collaborative relationships facilitate innovation by scaling up resources and capacity (O'Leary and Vij, 2012). The creation of new policy ideas, new technology, and new processes of service delivery consumes both fiscal resources and human capital for R&D, knowledge transfer, and large-scale implementation. Social network scholars find relationship building in networks and partner selection decisions are often driven by organizational leaders' assessment of common goals, shared ideas, and resource barriers (Smith, Huang, and Peng, 2020). Bringing multiple organizations together, networking and collaboration can scale up fiscal resources and human capital needed for innovation. By bringing different organizations together, collabora-tive networks can also improve resources and human capital for innovation by diversifying skill access. The resource effects of collaboration in networks have been well-documented in the past twenty years of public management research. In the analysis of governmental and nonprofit organizations' participation in collaborative water management initiatives in Florida, Berardo (2009) finds a positive association between the number of collaborative partners and the odds of successfully getting funded. Johansen and LeRoux (2013) studied more than 300 nonprofit organizations in sixteen American states. They find that funding resources increase as managerial efforts devoted to networking and collaboration. Scholars also find evidence that interorganizational collaboration mobilizes human capital in communities of practice (Agranoff, 2008) and helps to improve personnel stability in public and nonprofit organizations (Moynihan and Pandey, 2008).

Second, networking and collaboration can promote innovation by reducing the risk and costs associated with adopting new ideas and technology. Innovation can be risky and costly to organizations. The adoption of new technology and service process reforms often requires additional resources for personnel training. Public service innovation is also likely to face uncertainty related to the regulatory environment and citizen reactions. Existing research suggests that managers of service organizations can manage uncertainty through building and maintaining external networks with important stakeholders (Agranoff and McGuire, 1999; O'Toole, 1997), and creating interorganizational bonding with important policy stakeholders, clients, and peer organizations. Networking and collaboration can become an effective means to reduce external political uncertainty and to build mutual trust among peer organizations (Meier and O'Toole, 2001; O'Toole et al., 2006; O'Toole and Meier, 2011). Likewise, service organizations that engage in collaborative activities would face less uncertainty when undertaking innovation. Barrutia and Echebarria (2019) contribute new evidence regarding collaborative innovation in municipalities and find strong links between horizontal collaborative relationships (outward collaboration) cross-city governments and different types of innovation.

Furthermore, scholars find in various service areas that interorganizational collaboration offers channels for sharing information and knowledge as well as speeding up the diffusion of new knowledge, new technology, and new methods of service delivery (Cassel et al., 2018; Huang, 2014; Minstrom and Vergari, 1998; Moolenaar, Daly, and Sleegers, 2010; Provan et al.,2013). In their seminal work on the diffusion of state-level education reform in the USA, Minstrom and Vergari (1998) observe that states learn about policy innovation through their mutual connections in collaborative policy networks. Intergovernmental ties and horizontal connections increase the probability of adopting new education policies. Moolenaar, Daly, and Sleegers (2010) also focus on the education context by examining the interorganizational links between Dutch public schools. They find that interschool collaboration creates an innovative climate in schools, because collaborative ties provide an important forum for school principals in which to share knowledge about new education technology and experiences in curriculum reforms. Lieberman (2000) summarizes that, in the area of education, interorganizational collaboration creates a community of learning and disseminates innovative ideas and new technology.

Consistent evidence regarding networks and knowledge transfer also emerges from the health and human service context. Interorganizational collaboration not only becomes the locus of new knowledge creation, but also accelerates innovation transfer through learning and knowledge sharing (Powell, Koput, and Smith-Doerr, 1996). Knowledge sharing and technology transfer are both salient in health care networks. In their analysis of the network structure of the North American Quitline Consortium, Provan et al. (2013) find that intensive interorganizational interactions are positively associated with the sharing of new medical knowledge and evidence-based health service practices. Similarly, Huang (2014) suggests, service innovation in mental health care networks spread more efficiently through horizontal interorganization links than vertical contacts between member organizations and network-administration entities. In their study of more than 300 Californian hospitals over a ten-year period, Goes and Park (1997) find that hospitals are more likely to adopt service innovation when they are linked with other hospitals for shared administrative functions, collaborative interactions for resource exchange, and frequent interactions through common professional associations. The key conclusion from the health care networks literature is that innovation is enhanced by the development of interorganizational links and collaborative relationships. Cassel et al. (2018) report that partnership and frequent interactions with dedicated diffusion centers are key to the diffusion of palliative care innovation in the US hospital sector.

Last, but not least, collaborative networks can affect innovation activities by promoting the social norms of innovation. Through collaborative links, information about partner organizations' activities can spread through frequent interactions among top managers and network-level activities. The embedded relationships may produce forces to conform to collective action and increase institutional isomorphism. DiMaggio and Powell (1983) describe this mechanism as the "normative pressure" brought by professional associations and networks (p. 152). DiMaggio and Powell (1983) point out that service organizations in areas in which accurate pricing of service is difficult or impossible particularly need to invest in status competition and reputation management, because "organizational prestige and resources are key to attract professionals" (p. 154). For organizations that are mostly embedded in collaborative relationships, joining the coalition for innovation can bring them organizational reputation. For collaborative partners that share the same client and human capital pool, network participation can help organizations to learn their peers' behavior and new technology (Feiock, Lee, and Park, 2012; McKinney and Zuckerman, 1991), and motivate organizations to be more active in adopting service innovation.

Embedded in collaborative relationships, service organizations can also learn about one another's performative reputation (competency in achieving certain policy goals), moral reputation (the ability to represent and protect clients' interests), and procedural reputation (the ability to comply with new rules and procedures) (Moynihan, Carpenter, and Krause, 2012) in a speedy way. Horizontal alliances, especially multilateral partnerships, spread the reputation of being the cutting-edge service providers more quickly than isolated organizations. Likewise, organizations that are most embedded in collaborative networks might also bear the great reputational cost of being the laggards of innovation (Moynihan, Carpenter, and Krause, 2012; Schalk, Torenvlied, and Allen, 2010), because embedded social relations spread information about innovation to all networking partners.

To sum up, the existing literature suggests that interorganizational collaboration reduces the risk and uncertainty of innovation, expedites information and knowledge sharing regarding service and technology innovation, and spreads the norm of innovation. Because of these mechanisms, interorganizational collaboration is expected to spur innovation (Hartley, 2005; Hartley and Allison, 2002). *Compared to isolated monopoly, service organizations in a highly networked world would be more likely to engage with innovation activities.*

2.3 Collaboration in Competitive Environments: Coopetition and Innovation

Although past research has produced evidence on how interorganizational links increase collaboration, most of the existing studies in this area examine the impact of collaboration on innovation without considering the varying contexts of market competition. Overlooked in the literature is the more complex interorganizational dynamics, particularly the potential cross-pressure coming from competitive and collaborative relationships.

In fact, the link between competitive environment and innovation is one of the most debated themes in the New Public Management (NPM) literature. Influenced by the neoliberalism tradition and theories of rational firms, the NPM approach underpins the assumption that most service organizations are "customer" driven. In spite of their different legal ownerships, service organizations in all three sectors operate in some form of local markets, and often compete for clients, budget resources, and organizational reputation (Hartley and Allison, 2002). Innovation, therefore, is primarily driven by the need to seek a competitive advantage. For service organizations, innovation is both the creation of new knowledge and the ability to turn such new knowledge into profit or improved performance (Powell, Koput, and Smith-Doerr, 1996). In a competitive environment, organizations need to manage productivity and efficiency in service production and delivery. Because innovation is a key driver of productivity, external market competition is likely to drive organizations to focus more on service innovation and to restrict the sharing of new knowledge and new technology with partner organizations (Hartley, 2005). The private sector literature also suggests that through innovation, a slack-related concern, organizations can seize greater market share or to expand into new markets (Greve, 2003).

Similarly, many nonprofit and public organizations are constrained by market conditions, because they cannot shift service markets, and they are often imposed with goals in producing public services and improving performance outcomes for citizens (Brown and Osborne, 2013). For them, gaining competitive advantage by improving performance is indicative to additional budget resources and autonomy in the use of these resources (Meier, Favero, and Zhu, 2015). Although innovation (such as investment in research and new technologies) can be costly in the short term, it is expected to generate better performance and to increase organizational autonomy in the public and nonprofit sectors. Therefore, facing competitive pressure in the local market, public and nonprofit organizations are also more likely to innovate.

Nevertheless, more recent studies on market competition and innovation challenge the conventional wisdom that the relationship between competition and innovation is monotonically positive. Aghion et al. (2005) investigate the inverted-U relationship between competition and changes in the number of firm patents in UK. They find that when the competition is low and moderate, technology innovation activities increase, but the pace of innovation declines as the level of competition becomes very high. Uyarra et al. (2014) find the public procurement contracting process benefits larger contractors more than small contractors regarding their propensity of innovation, because the latter group is often more constrained by fierce rivalry pressures. The pattern that highly competitive market environment has a chilling effect on innovation is confirmed by US data on industrial organizations (Hashimi, 2013). These recent studies demonstrate the need to further explore how interorganizational dynamics may affect organizational behavior in highly competitive market environments.

While both market competition and network collaboration are key drivers of innovation, they do not necessarily operate as separate forces. Instead, collaborative relationships may indirectly influence innovation through organizations' external market constraints. Because neither market nor networks can fully capture how organizations interact with each other, the concept of coopetition, namely, the coexistence of competition and collaboration, has gained traction among organizational behavior scholars. Research on coopetition has emerged as a new direction to study interorganizational dynamics, yet the majority of this literature is still theoretical and qualitative (Devece et al., 2019). Main insights from the coopetition literature inform us that knowledge-intensive and human-capital-intensive service areas (e.g., education, health care, social services, etc.) are often characterized by the presence of both competition and collaboration (Barretta, 2008). A competitive service market often motivates service organizations to pursue greater efficiency. However, innovation can be costly in a short term, which constrains organizations from giving high priority to R&D or radical technology innovation. Research also suggests that there may be a nonlinear relationship between innovation and performance. Innovation may initially decrease performance, but pay off more fully in the future (Chen, 2008; Meier, Favero, and Zhu, 2015). Therefore, when organizations are facing high pressures of improving performance (e.g., those from a high-stake performance appraisal system), they may be constrained from investing in innovation. The paradox here is that, on the one hand, competition creates the need to innovate and change, but, on the other hand, resource and performance considerations may prevent some organizations from becoming leaders in innovation.

Networking and collaboration can free organizations from these constraints when they are taking the initiatives of innovation. Through collaboration with competitors that are rivals for the same clientele pool, cost and risks of innovation, particularly major innovations, are shared among partner organizations rather than being shouldered by an organization by itself. Moreover, because most service organizations are customer-oriented, citizens are usually deemed to have a larger role as coproducers of service and innovation. Through networking and collaboration, partner organizations can increase their total capacity to serving more diverse clients, and improve the coproduction process, through which they gain external support on innovation, additional resources for policy experiments, and new models of service delivery (Hartley, 2005). As such, when organizations are embedded in a highly competitive market environment, they may be motivated to innovate, but through network collaboration, their actual capacity of innovation can be strengthened. Qualitative studies provide suggestive evidence that coopetition between organizations better motivates innovation than competitive pressures simply coming from the market (LeTourneau, 2004; Yami and Nemeh, 2014).

Scholars also find, compared with neck-to-neck competition, coopetition may accelerate innovation through diversified knowledge and the cumulation of social capital within the socially embedded relationships between organizations. In their study of innovation in the high-technology industry, Ritala and Hurmelinna-Laukkanen (2009) find that collaboration with competitors, especially the formation of multilateral coopetition, enable collective value creation. As the number of partners increases in the network of coopetition, interorganizational trust and the diversification of knowledge will also increase (Dyer and Singh, 1998). Both interorganizational trust and diversity of knowledge sources are intangible assets for driving innovation activities, which are difficult to be implemented in neck-to-neck competition and zero-sum games.

In their study of higher education institutions in Europe, Bennett and Kottasz (2011) find that universities compete fiercely for students, while collaborating on recruiting international students, research, library access, and jointly trialing out new approaches of innovation. They also highlight the difference between coopetition and sheer collaboration. Universities in pure collaborative relationships usually have complementary students (clientele) pools, while coopetition is found among universities sharing the similar clientele pool. The presence of competition within a collaborative network, according to Bennett and Kottasz (2011), will also increase the attempt to develop service specialization to maintain their relative status and reputation. As such, the coopetition relationship will magnify the motivation for innovation in a more salient way than sheer collaboration. Similar evidence is found in Muijs and Rumyantseva's (2014) qualitative study of six English colleges, which finds competition and collaboration jointly inform curriculum innovation and speed up high-quality professional development.

Addressing the nonprofit and health care sector, McCarthy et al. (2018) find similar evidence that coopetition accelerates innovation by increasing and diversifying knowledge stocks, increasing knowledge exchange, and cultivating trust. Examining the ten-year experience of building collaborative ties among eight large nonprofit hospitals that compete with each other at the national level, McCarthy et al. (2018) find that the simultaneous presence of competitive and collaborative relationships among these large health care providers motivate leaders' continuing search for innovation as means to maintain their organization's competitive advantage. Meanwhile, networking and collaboration catalyze knowledge sharing by minimizing the fear of idea-stealing between competitors (p. 28). Coopetition also leads to the adoption of formal mechanisms for teaching/transferring innovation experiences within single organizations, resulting in greater collective competency in innovation. McCarthy et al. (2018, p. 33) conclude that "competition is a traditional force for improvement and innovation, coopetition is emerging as a new way to tackle complexity" and to produce more rapid innovation.

Focusing on the Dutch health care context, van Den Broek et al. (2018) find that, as Dutch hospitals are facing increasing competition, innovation slows down due to scarcity in financial resources and the difficulty of retaining talented employees. Their case study report evidence that coopetition between four hospitals in the same regional service market formed a "joint Talent Management Pool", which, in turn, helped competitors to maintain collective consumption of human capital. In this case, coopetition promotes innovation in competitive environments by solving problems of resource shortage due to intensive competition.

Although empirical studies on coopetition in public service are still limited in numbers and primarily contribute qualitative evidence. These studies clearly suggest that coopetition differs from collaboration. Considering the interplay between interorganizational collaboration and competition, one can expect that *organizations with a high level of coopetition are more likely to innovate than isolated organizations facing a low level of competition, or organizations that are only embedded in competitive relationships.*

3 Coopetition and the Adoption of New Medical Technology

The American health care sector provides an excellent empirical context to examine how the interplay between interorganizational competition and collaboration affect innovation. The American health care sector is a mixed-ownership fee-for-service system, which includes hospitals from the public, nonprofit, and for-profit sectors. Different from many European countries that have universal health insurance systems and more coordinated hospital sectors, the US health care system is fragmented, large in the number of insurance and care providers, and is a hotbed for intertwined interorganization competition and collaboration.

Public, nonprofit, and for-profit hospitals, although differing in their legal ownership, produce and deliver services based on the same medical industry standards. Hospitals from the same area often engage in interorganizational collaborations for more effective service delivery. Meanwhile, hospitals in the same local area compete with each other for government funding, patients (especially Medicare patients), and health care professionals. The complex interorganizational dynamics offer a rich empirical context to validate measures of interorganizational competition and collaboration. Westra et al. (2017) find cooperative interorganizational relations are salient in health care delivery and often occur among hospitals in price-competitive market segments.

Examining coopetition and innovation in the health care sector is also practically important. In the USA, health care is the largest service sector by its economic scale and the publicness of its funding sources. According to the Centers of Medicare & Medicaid Services (CMS) National Health Expenditure data, US health care spending reached $3.6 trillion in 2018, and accounted for 17.7 percent of the nation's gross domestic product (GDP) (Hartman et al., 2020), one-third of which was spending on hospital care. Regardless of the legal ownership, government-owned hospitals, nonprofit hospitals, and private hospitals all rely on public funding sources, such as Medicare and Medicaid. In 2018, Medicare and Medicaid together accounted for 38 percent of the total US health care spending (Hartman et al., 2020). The share of health care spending in national GDP is projected to increase by a steady annual rate of 5.4 percent in the next ten years (Keehan et al. 2020).

Health care, as a major public service area in the USA, is also marked with heavy investment in medical health research and development (R&D) and various forms of service innovation (Balas and Chapman, 2018). In 2018, the total medical health R&D investment was near $194 billion, of which the private sector invested about two-thirds, and the federal government invested over 22 percent (Keehan et al., 2020). The adoption of medical and service innovation, however, has proved to be uneven across different local health care markets. As Gee (2000) describes, while many theoretical discussions have been written about coopetition, research on coopetition and innovation in the health care context is still limited. Existing research on coopetition in health care remains fragmented and mostly qualitative (McCarthy et al., 2018). The US health care sector is an area ripe for the empirical application of the coopetition framework. In this section, I explore how the interplay of competition and collaboration is linked to innovation, focusing on the adoption of new medical technology in the hospital sector.

3.1 Panel Data Design

Data used in the empirical models are drawn from the American Hospital Association (AHA) Annual Hospital Survey (AHS) Database, which is the most reliable and accurate data source about American hospitals' organizational characteristics, collaborative activities, and organizational behavior involving service and technology innovation. Because the AHA is the national professional association of hospitals in the USA, the AHA survey has a very high average response rate (around 75 percent) across years. The AHA Annual Hospital Survey Database produces nationally representative annual samples to mirror key organizational characteristics of the entire US hospital population (6,000+ hospitals), such as organizational ownership, hospital size, geographic area, and service specialization. The AHA collects data from its member hospitals using its online survey platform. A mail-based survey is used as the supplementary mode to boost survey participation and reduce attrition across the years. Responses to the AHA annual survey are certified by each hospital's CEO or CIO. Information regarding hospitals' basic characteristics is cross-validated with the CMS database on hospitals that provide services to Medicare patients. The AHA Annual Hospital Survey is well recognized and used by scholars in health care innovation (Goes and Park, 1997), health care manage-ment, and health care policy (Johansen and Zhu, 2014; Zhu, 2017). Government agencies such as the US Centers for Medicare and Medicaid Services (CMS) also rely on the AHA survey data to track major trends in the hospital industry.

Drawing from the AHA Annual Hospital Survey Database, I constructed a panel dataset of more than 4,000 hospitals from 2008 to 2017. Longitudinal repeated measures of hospitals make it possible to track innovation activities that occur in different years while controlling for common national trends in innovation due to changes in national health care policies and population demographics. Empirical data on the past decade also provide a timely analysis of most recent changes in health care service markets and innovation activities during the national health care reform under the Patient Protection and Affordable Care Act of 2010.

Table 1 summarizes the basic characteristics of hospitals included in the panel dataset. Public hospitals owned by federal, state, county governments, and local health districts approximately accounted for 25 percent of the American hospitals in 2008, which decreased to around 21.2 percent in 2017. The nonprofit sector dominates the hospital industry by the sheer number of hospitals. Nonprofit hospitals in the USA refer to church-operated and other non-governmental nonprofit hospitals. They are governed by the IRS 501(c)(3) requirements for tax exemption, including required community health needs assessment (CHNA), financial assistance and emergency medical care policy, limitation on service charges, and rules regarding billing and collection. Nonprofit hospitals account for more than 55 percent of in-samples cases. Private hospitals refer to hospitals that are owned by individuals, private physician partnerships, and corporations. Also included in this category are investor-owned for-profits. They operate in the same way as business firms. This sector accounts for about 20 percent of US hospitals.

Table 1 also shows the proportion of rural hospitals in the empirical sample. Rural hospitals are defined based on the US Census Bureau Core-Based Statistical Areas (CBSA). Hospitals in a CBSA type of "division" or "metro" are classified as urban hospitals and in a CBSA type of "rural" or "micropolitan" are defined as rural hospitals. By this classification, over one-third of the American hospitals are rural hospitals in areas with low population density.

Table 1 Characteristics of in-sample hospitals, 2008–2017

Year	N	% Public hospital	% Nonprofit hospital	% Private hospital	% Rural hospital	Average size (FTE)
2008	4,844	24.9%	55.9%	19.2%	37.9%	907
2009	4,768	24.2%	56.1%	19.7%	37.4%	925
2010	4,793	23.8%	55.6%	20.6%	36.8%	926
2011	4,799	22.8%	56.1%	21.1%	36.5%	940
2012	4,793	22.6%	55.9%	21.5%	36.8%	949
2013	4,789	21.5%	56.9%	21.6%	35.8%	959
2014	4,622	21.5%	57.0%	21.5%	34.6%	975
2015	4,751	21.5%	56.4%	22.1%	33.9%	990
2016	4,613	20.6%	57.0%	22.4%	34.2%	1,031
2017	4,288	21.2%	59.5%	19.3%	34.7%	1,100

Data source: American Hospital Annual Survey Database.

The share of rural hospitals decreased during the past decade, from 37.9 percent in 2008 to 34.7 percent in 2017.

Based on the number of fulltime-equivalent employees, the average size of American hospitals was slightly over 900 employees, which increased to over 1,100 in 2017. Hospital size also varies substantially. The largest in-sample hospital in 2017 had more than 30,000 employees.

3.2 The Adoption of New Medical Technology

The subsequent analysis focuses on the adoption of new medical technology as an innovation activity. In their recent literature review on public service innovation, Vries, Sekker, and Tummers (2016) point out that innovation is an expansive concept. The literature on public service innovation covers a wide range of innovation activities, including process innovation, administrative process innovation, technology innovation, product or service innovation, governance innovation, and conceptual innovation. Based on this typology, technology innovation refers to the creation or adoption of new technology by an organization to deliver services to clients (Vries, Bekkers and Tummers, 2016). A large amount of existing research on public sector innovation has been devoted to e-government, the adoption of information technology, and the digital transformation of service delivery (Wang and Feeney, 2014; West, 2004).

The health care sector has followed the same trend of technology innovation and witnessed the adoption and diffusion of electronic health records (EHRs). There is a wide consensus that the use of electronic health information technology, similar to the e-government movement in other public service areas, should lead to the safe storage of patient records, more efficient exchange of patient information, synchronized knowledge sharing across hospitals, physicians and other care providers, and improved quality of care (Jha et al., 2009). Considering this salient trend of technology innovation, I gathered data on the adoption of EHRs across American hospitals from 2008 to 2017 as the first empirical measure for the adoption of new medical technology. In the subsequent analysis, this measure is operationalized based on the AHA survey question, asking if a hospital has adopted an EHR system in a given year. Responses are coded as a dichotomous variable, with "1" referring to the full adoption of an EHR system and "0" otherwise.

Beyond the adoption of EHRs, I also include two additional measures to track the adoption of robotic surgery and virtual reality technology in hospitals. Robot-assisted surgery was in its infancy and research phase in the mid-1980s. Since the late 1990s, the adoption of robotic surgery has taken expanded at an unprecedented rate in the USA and Europe after the Da Vinci robotic system entered into its full marketing stage (Mele et al., 2013). The US hospital sector has the greatest number of surgical robots in the world, with a high concentration of robotic surgery services in nonprofit and public hospitals. The AHA continuously surveys its member hospitals regarding whether robot-assisted surgery has been adopted, producing longitudinal binary data on the adoption of robotic surgery.

I consider the adoption of virtual reality (VR) simulation technology as the third innovation variable. Similarly to robotic surgery, the use of virtual reality technology in health care took off in the late 1990s. The core application areas of VR technology in health care include a simulation-based environment for rehabilitation therapy and the use of VR simulations in medical education (Moline, 1997). Similarly to both EHRs and robotic surgery, VR simulations are thought to be new technology that will change the way in which health care services are delivered to patients and how medical knowledge is taught in teaching hospitals. The empirical measure of this technology innovation activity is also operationalized based on the AHA annual survey question regarding if a hospital has adopted VR simulation-based rehabilitation service in a given year. The three technology innovation activities share some common features. First, they all utilize new advancements in computer and informatics technology in the process of delivering health care services. Second, they are all high-cost innovation activities, characterized by high fixed capital costs for equipment acquisition and high operating costs due to equipment maintenance and the training of surgeons and other specialized personnel. Third, the major motivation of adopting these medical technologies is to improve service efficiency and patient outcomes.

Nevertheless, electronic health records, virtual reality technology, and surgical robots are promoted by different stakeholder in the health care sector. EHRs have been heavily promoted and funded by the federal government since the Bush administration. Under the American Recovery and Reinvestment Act of 2009, all health care providers are mandated to adopt a certified EHR system, with Medicare funding penalty for noncompliance. Differently from EHRs, by way of contrast, the adoption of surgical robots and VR technology are much more driven by the market force and evidence-based planning in both the United States (Blute and Prestipino, 2014) and Europe (Mele et al., 2014). Analyzing these different technology innovations rather than focusing on one single technology may provide more generalizable evidence regarding how coopeting may drive innovation.

Table 2 presents the trends of medical technology adoption in these three areas. Between 2008 and 2017, the adoption of robotic surgery and VR

Table 2 Adoption of medical robots, virtual reality technology, and electronic health records in American hospitals, 2008–2017

Year	% Hospitals adopted robotic surgery	N	% Hospitals adopted simulated rehabilitation environment	N	% Hospitals adopted EHR	N
2008	11.8%	4,844	17.0%	4,705	17.5%	4,180
2009	14.8%	4,768	20.1%	4,768	20.3%	4,134
2010	17.1%	4,793	22.6%	4,793	29.1%	3,290
2011	20.3%	4,799	23.8%	4,799	33.2%	4,047
2012	23.1%	4,793	24.7%	4,793	43.5%	4,150
2013	25.3%	4,789	25.8%	4,792	56.1%	4,046
2014	27.5%	4,622	26.7%	4,622	66.6%	3,895
2015	28.4%	4,751	27.4%	4,751	73.9%	3,964
2016	30.4%	4,613	29.4%	4,613	77.9%	4,021
2017	32.3%	4,288	30.4%	4,288	–	–

Data source: American Hospital Association Annual Hospital Survey Database. Data regarding EHR adoption are not available in the 2017 AHA survey.

technology exhibits the pattern of incremental growth. In 2008, about 11 percent of hospitals had adopted robotic surgery and 17 percent of hospitals had adopted VR technology to provide simulation-based rehabilitation therapy. In 2017, the adoption rate in these two areas became near one-third. To date, the majority of hospitals have still not adopted these two medical technologies.

In contrast, the adoption of EHRs has taken a different pace. The adoption of EHRs was quite limited in 2008. Only about 17.5 percent of American hospitals had fully upgraded their paper-based medical records into an electronic health information system. EHR adoption accelerated after the passage of the Health Information Technology for Economic and Clinical Health (HITECH) Act of 2009. By 2014, across all states, at least half of hospitals had adopted a basic EHR system. Influenced by federal legislations and fiscal incentives, the diffusion of EHRs was also more quickly in public and nonprofit hospitals than that in the for-profit sector. In 2016, nearly 80 percent of public hospitals and 84 percent of nonprofit hospitals adopted EHRs. The adoption rate was only about 55 percent among private for-profit hospitals. For robotic surgery and VR technology, hospitals across the three sectors have comparable adoption rates.

3.3 Inter-Hospital Competition, Collaboration, and Coopetition

To develop systematic quantitative analyses of how variations in adopting new medical technology might be attributed to the different scenarios of interorganizational interactions, I validate measures of market competition, inter-hospital collaboration, and then examined the interplay between competition and collaboration.

Measuring Market Competition.   Following prior research on health care market competition (Baker,2001; Johansen and Zhu, 2014; Robinson, 2011), I conceptualize the level of market competition faced by a hospital in its local health care market based on two factors commonly used in the health economics literature: the availability of similar health care providers in an area, and the degree of market-share concentration in that local service area. I use the AHA/ Dartmouth Hospital service area (HSA) code to pinpoint the geographic boundary of hospitals' local service market. HAS codes assign all hospitals to a city or town based on their geographical location. Then a cluster of ZIP codes within a city or town are linked to hospitals most often used by local residents. The resulting geographic delineation (HSAs) contains a set of ZIP codes based on Medicare hospitalization records (Hu et al., 2018). HSAs balance the physical location of hospitals and the patient utilization records in drawing geographic boundaries of hospital service markets. I then divide each HSA into two market niches based on hospitals' specialization type, resulting in one market for general hospitals and one market niche for specialized hospitals within each HSA. The consideration is that hospitals compete in the same local service area for clients and core fiscal resources, but only directly with those who provide mutually substitutable services.

I then calculate a *market competition* index based on a rescaled Herfindahl-Hirschman Index (HHI), capturing the concentration of health care services in hospitals' local health care markets. Within each market niche, I quantifiedy the competition index based on Equation (1). S_{ij} denotes each hospital's market share of total health care service outputs across total outpatient visits, inpatient surgeries, and outpatient surgeries. Summing ($\sum$) the S_{ij}^2 term in each local market area produces an HHI of market concentration that is bounded between 0 and 1, where one refers to a monopolized local market in which all the emergency care, inpatient, and outpatient services are concentrated in one hospital. I then subtract the HHI from 1 to obtain the market competition scale, such that a value of 0 indicates a hospital monopoly facing no competition in the local market, and values near 1 represent intense competition in a local market (McCrea and Zhu, 2019).

$$\text{Competition index} = 1 - \sum (S_{ij}^2) \tag{1}$$

Measuring Inter-Hospital Collaboration. Inter-hospital collaboration is assessed based on horizontal alliances between hospitals. American hospitals build formal collaborative partnerships with peer hospitals through three modes: participating in a hospital system, participating in a hospital network, or forming a joint venture (Bazzoli et al., 1999). A hospital system usually only includes partner hospitals, while a hospital network connects multiple hospitals with other health care organizations such as long-term care facilities and nurse groups. Hospital joint ventures operate similarly to other business joint ventures. In spite of the different forms, inter-hospital collaboration in these networked relationships is formal and mostly horizontal. To empirically measure the intensity of inter-hospital collaboration in these networked relationships, I focus on collaboration activities in service delivery.

The AHA dataset provides comprehensive information on the method of service provision across more than 150 specific health care services, ranging from general primary care, various surgical operations/procedures, intensive care units, walking therapy, pain-alleviation therapy, diagnostic screenings, to auxiliary services such as meals on wheels. For the full inventory of health care services, hospitals report to the AHA annually about whether they provide each service in-house or through participation in a local health care network, local health care system, or a joint venture. I calculate the inter-hospital *collaboration* scale based on the proportion of hospital services provided through the collaborative model (i.e., via a health care network, system, or a joint venture). This collaboration scale ranges from 0 to 1, which essentially reflects the intensity of collaborative service provision through hospitals' participation in collaborative networks. It is worth noting that the collaboration scale measures hospitals' formal partnerships with peer hospitals.

Table 3 summarizes the trends of mean competition and collaboration scores by sector. During the past decade, the mean competition scores in hospitals' local health care markets exhibited stability across years, but sizable differences across the three sectors. On average, government-owned hospitals face relatively low market competition, which the private for-profit sector is featured with high competition. The trends of inter-hospital collaboration for service delivery also shows interesting cross-sector differences. On average, collaborative service delivery is higher among nonprofit hospitals than that in the public sector and for-profit sector. Nonprofit and private hospitals, furthermore, experienced steady increases in collaborative service provision.

Using the market competition scale and inter-hospital collaboration scale, I further assessed the proportion of hospitals in each sector that are experiencing high competition and high collaboration simultaneously. In Table 3, The "coopetition" scenario is approximated based on finding hospitals that have competition and collaboration scores greater than the corresponding sample medians. By this approximation, Table 3 shows some interesting patterns. Coopetition appears to be a more prevalent phenomenon in the nonprofit sector, followed by the for-profit sector. Near half of the nonprofit hospitals experience high inter-hospital competition and collaborative service provision simultaneously. Both public hospital sector and for-profit hospital sector include nearly 1,500 hospitals. Over 35 percent of for-profit hospitals and about 20 percent of public hospitals are in the coopetition scenario.

3.4 Inter-Hospital Dynamics and the Adoption of New Medical Technology

I estimated a set of panel logistic regression models to further explore how variations in competition, collaboration, and coopetition shape the adoption of new medical technology. In the empirical analysis, I controlled for hospitals' organizational characteristics. First, I controlled for hospital size measured by hospitals' inpatient bed capacity and FTE. The bed-capacity variable was based on the AHA's standard bed-capacity category, measured as a 1 to 8 ordinal scale. Category 1 refers to small hospitals that have fewer than twenty-five inpatient

Table 3 Trends of competition, collaboration, and coopetition among American hospitals

Year	Mean competition score			Mean collaboration score			Percent in coopetition		
	Public	Nonprofit	Private	Public	Nonprofit	Private	Public	Nonprofit	Private
2008	0.259	0.289	0.449	0.155	0.232	0.188	20%	44.8%	35.1%
2009	0.260	0.287	0.444	0.164	0.245	0.198	21%	44.3%	34.3%
2010	0.251	0.283	0.416	0.162	0.245	0.187	20%	45.3%	34.4%
2011	0.254	0.284	0.413	0.165	0.251	0.202	19.7%	47.7%	33.6%
2012	0.253	0.280	0.408	0.172	0.264	0.200	19.7%	46.4%	33.9%
2013	0.249	0.278	0.410	0.167	0.263	0.207	19.3%	45.7%	35.0%
2014	0.248	0.278	0.404	0.177	0.274	0.213	19.1%	45.3%	35.5%
2015	0.243	0.279	0.407	0.182	0.284	0.218	18.1%	45.8%	36.1%
2016	0.241	0.275	0.409	0.188	0.292	0.226	18.2%	45.6%	36.1%
2017	0.248	0.277	0.417	0.198	0.321	0.245	18.1%	45.8%	36.1%

Data source: American Hospital Association Annual Hospital Survey Database.

beds, and category 8 refers to large hospitals with 500 or more beds. The average hospital bed-size category is 3.54, corresponding approximately to 150 beds.

Second, to account for cross-sector differences in management practice (Johansen and Zhu, 2014) and different market pressures due to service specialization, I included a few dummy variables to control for hospitals' legal ownership and service specialization. In the empirical models, three dummy variables are included for public hospitals, nonprofit hospitals, and general hospitals. I also controlled for rural hospitals and hospitals' medical school affiliations, as hospitals in rural areas are less likely to engage in service innovation, and university-affiliated hospitals are often the leaders in technology research and development.

Because the three technology innovation variables were coded as dichotomous variables, I estimated three sets of dynamic panel logistic regressions. Two different model specifications were considered and reported in the subsequent empirical tables: the baseline specification without year-fixed effects and the alternative specification with a full set of year-fixed effects to control for unobserved national trends due to changes in federal legislation and population demographic trends. The year-dummy variable specification is to follow Beck, Katz, and Tucker (1998)'s recommendation that cross-section time-series data with binary outcome variables can be treated as group-duration data. Adding a series of year-fixed effects to account for duration dependence is an appealing strategy, particularly when the CSTS data are featured with a small T (Beck, Katz, and Tucker, 1998). Carter and Signorino (2010) sound a cautionary note that when analyzing CSTS data with binary outcomes, including time dummies may cause the issue of separation. They recommend an alternative specification strategy: replacing time dummies with t, t2, and t3 in the regression model. I conducted a robustness check using the Carter and Signorino (2010) empirical strategy, which did not find substantively different results. In addition, the concept of coopetition centers on the interplay between competition and collaboration, I included a multiplicative term between *competition* and *collaboration* in the empirical analysis.

Table 4 presents panel logistic regression models for the three technology innovation variables. Models (1), (3), and (5) are three baseline models without the interaction term between *competition* and *collaboration*, and without year-fixed effects. Models (2), (4), and (6) are full models, including both the interaction term for coopetition and year-fixed effects.

Across the six models, there is no evidence that sheer market competition drives up the adoption of new medical technology. In the three baseline models, furthermore, the coefficients *inter-hospital collaboration*, are consistently

Table 4 Coopetition and the adoption of new medical technology in American hospitals, 2008–2017: Panel logistic regression models

VARIABLES	(1) Robotic surgery	(2) Robotic surgery	(3) VR technology	(4) VR technology	(5) EHR	(6) EHR
Competition	−0.037	−0.376***	−0.372***	−0.481***	−0.028	0.012
	(0.047)	(0.074)	(0.038)	(0.053)	(0.038)	(0.061)
Collaboration	0.528***	−0.358***	0.108**	−0.148**	0.971***	0.706***
	(0.069)	(0.101)	(0.052)	(0.075)	(0.053)	(0.082)
Competition X collaboration	—	1.630***	—	0.478***	—	0.333**
		(0.189)		(0.190)		(0.158)
Public hospital	−1.290***	−1.278***	−0.284***	−0.260***	0.365***	0.583***
	(0.061)	(0.062)	(0.040)	(0.040)	(0.039)	(0.044)
Nonprofit hospital	−0.339***	−0.309***	0.186***	0.206***	0.370***	0.560***
	(0.041)	(0.043)	(0.033)	(0.034)	(0.035)	(0.039)
General hospital	1.954***	2.058***	−0.219***	−0.221***	0.887***	1.139***
	(0.068)	(0.071)	(0.034)	(0.035)	(0.038)	(0.045)
Rural hospital	−1.159***	−1.214***	−0.330***	−0.333***	−0.265***	−0.295***
	(0.045)	(0.046)	(0.032)	(0.032)	(0.029)	(0.033)
Medical school	−0.075**	−0.024	−0.261***	−0.244***	−0.354***	−0.332***
	(0.036)	(0.037)	(0.030)	(0.030)	(0.030)	(0.034)
Bed capacity	0.470***	0.537***	0.278***	0.290***	−0.019*	0.034***

Table 4 (cont.)

VARIABLES	(1) Robotic surgery	(2) Robotic surgery	(3) VR technology	(4) VR technology	(5) EHR	(6) EHR
	(0.016)	(0.017)	(0.010)	(0.010)	(0.010)	(0.011)
FTE	0.001***	0.001***	0.0002***	0.0002***	0.000***	0.000***
	(0.00001)	(0.00001)	(0.00001)	(0.00001)	(0.000)	(0.000)
Constant	−4.846***	−6.474***	−1.623***	−2.149***	−0.777***	−2.820***
	(0.121)	(0.146)	(0.079)	(0.092)	(0.082)	(0.104)
Year-fixed effects	No	Yes	No	Yes	No	Yes
observations	46,114	46,114	46,114	46,114	35,506	35,506

Robust standard errors in parentheses.

*** p< 0.01, ** p< 0.05, * p< 0.1

positive and statistically significant, indicating that the adoption of technology innovation might be higher in hospitals with high-interhospital collaboration than that among silo organizations. Models (2), (4), and (6) report consistent findings that the interaction term between *competition* and *collaboration* has a positive and statistically significant coefficient, suggesting the interplay between competition and collaboration significantly drives up the adoption of new medical technology.

Figure 2 visualizes the odds ratio coefficients based on the three interaction models in Table 4. Odds ratios for *competition*, *collaboration*, and *coopetition* are placed together with the odds ratio coefficients for rural hospital and bed-size capacity as comparisons. These odds ratio coefficients show the odds that the adoption of a specific technology innovation will occur under the condition of competition, collaboration, and coopetition respectively, compared to the odds of adopting the innovation in the absence of these conditions. Figure 2 shows a clear comparison that neither competition nor collaboration alone drives up the adoption of new medical technology. Instead, the interaction between competition and collaboration has a substantial impact on technology innovation. Based on Table 4, Model (2), the interaction term "Competition X collaboration" has a odds ratio coefficient of 5.1 ($p < 0.01$), meaning that hospitals in the coopetition scenario (i.e., facing high competition and

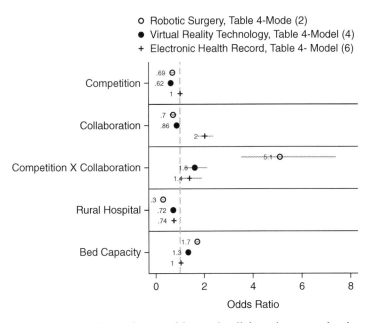

Figure 2 Joint effects of competition and collaboration on technology innovation

collaboration simultaneously) have significantly higher probability of adopting robotic surgery than monopolist hospitals without engaging in any inter-hospital collaboration in service delivery. Compared with isolated monopolies, hospitals with coopetition are four times more likely to adopt robotic surgery. Models (4) and (6) show the similar pattern that coopetition is associated with increased probability of adopting VR technology and EHRs. Comparing the odds ratio coefficients in Figure 2, coopetition is associated with effect sizes greater than that of hospital size (bed capacity) and inter-hospital collaboration alone.

Figure 3 visualizes key findings regarding competition, collaboration, and coopetition based on predicted probabilities of adopting robotic surgery. The visualization is produced by using Monte Carlo simulations and out-sample predictions to show how the predicted probability of adopting robotic surgery changes across the full observed range of the collaboration variable (King et al., 2000; Tomz et al., 2003). The mean predicted probabilities and the corresponding 95 percent confidence intervals are calculated for the scenarios of low- and high-inter hospital competition, defined by the 10th and 90th percentile of the competition scale. All the other explanatory variables are held constant at their sample medians. As such, Figure 3 maps on the four theoretical scenarios of inter-hospital relationships discussed in the previous section. In Figure 3, the

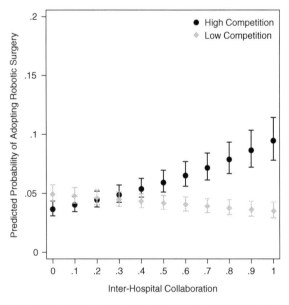

Figure 3 Collaboration and the adoption of robotic surgery in low and high market competition; visual based on Table 4, Model **(2)**

low market competition scenario represents hospitals with a competition score of 0 (i.e., no competition), across the full range of the inter-hospital collaboration scale. Moving from no collaboration to high collaboration reflects the comparison between the scenario of "isolated monopoly" and the scenario of "highly networked world." The predicted probability of adopting robotic surgery remains constantly low with a mean predicted probability of 0.05. This suggests, inter-hospital collaboration alone does not drive up the adoption of robotic surgery.

Using the same methods, Figure 4 visualizes the interactive effects of competition and collaboration on the adoption of VR technology. The different nuance shown in Figure 4 is that, in the absence of inter-hospital collaboration, the probability of adopting of VR technology is slightly higher when market competition is low than when market competition is high. Nevertheless, high competition combined with high collaboration is associated with higher probability of adoption than that in the scenario of neck-to-neck competition without collaboration. Figure 4 shows the case in which competitive environments hinder rather than promote technology innovation. Coopetition, however, promotes the adoption of VR technology in competitive environments.

Figure 5 adds consistent evidence regarding how coopetition drives the adoption of EHRs, based on Table 4, Model (6). As Figure 5 shows, the average

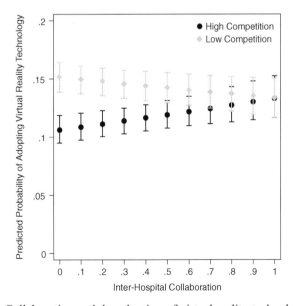

Figure 4 Collaboration and the adoption of virtual reality technology in low and high market competition; visual based on Table 4, Model **(4)**

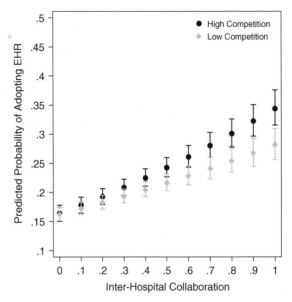

Figure 5 Collaboration and the adoption of electronic health record systems in low and high market competition; visual based on Table 4, Model **(6)**

predicted probability of adopting EHRs is low (0.15) in the scenario of isolated monopoly and neck-to-neck competition. Again, this is the case wherein competitive pressures from the local service markets do not translate into higher probabilities of adopting technology innovation. Regardless of the level of market competition, inter-hospital collaboration is associated with higher probabilities of adoption, suggesting the pattern of collaborative innovation (Hartley, Sorensen, and Torfing, 2013). Comparing the predicted probabilities of adopting EHRs when collaboration is high and in the two market competition scenarios, furthermore, Figure 5 shows the probability of adoption is higher when high competition and high collaboration exist simultaneously. The probability of adoption is around 0.25 when collaboration is high and competition is low, which increases to 0.35 under the condition of coopetition. Figures 3, 4, and 5, taken together, show a consistent pattern that the probability of adopting of new medical technology is always higher under coopetition than that in neck-to-neck competition and when a hospital is isolated monopoly.

A quick review of the control variables in Table 4 reveals findings as expected that hospital characteristics also partially explain their technology innovation activities. The adoption of expensive medical new technology is more prevalent in large hospitals than in small hospitals. Both bed-size capacity and human resources are positively associated with the adoption of new medical technology. Rural hospitals are significantly less innovative than urban hospitals. Compared with specialized hospitals, general hospitals are more likely to adopt robotic surgery and EHRs, but slightly less likely to adopt virtual reality technology. This is because a large proportion of general hospitals do not provide rehabilitation services and are not affiliated with medical schools. There are also salient cross-sector differences regarding the baseline adoption rate. Compared with private for-profit hospitals, public and nonprofit hospitals are more likely to adopt EHRs and virtual reality technology, but less likely to purchase medical robots.

4 Collaboration and Service Innovation in Competitive Markets

In the previous section, I explored empirically how competition, collaboration, and coopetition shaped the adoption of new medical technology in the American health care sector during the past decade. In this section, I continue on examining the nexus of competition and collaboration and the adoption of service innovation. Service innovation refers to the creation of a new service or the adoption of new processes for delivering public service (Vries et al., 2016; Walker, 2014). The empirical analysis in this section centers on the adoption of two service innovations – mobile health services and telemedicine.

According to the AHA definition, mobile health services, also called mobile health clinics (MHCs), refer to the use of vans and other vehicles for providing primary care services. It is an innovative model of health service delivery by sending physicians and health care professionals into communities, instead of the traditional model of health care provision in hospital facilities (Yu et al., 2017). MHCs hold great promise in expanding access to primary care and preventive screening in high vulnerability populations at a low cost. It is estimated that more than 5 million primary care visits are delivered through MHCs, most of which concentrate in low-income communities, rural areas, and immigrant communities (Edgerley et al., 2007). Similar to MHCs, telemedicine is also an innovative service provision model using telecommunication technologies to improve access to care and the outreach to patients at relatively low costs (Ekeland, Bowes, and Flottorp, 2010). Interests in adopting telemedicine began to increase in the health care sector in the 1990s. During the same decade, the US federal government and state governments began to increase budget incentives for telemedicine demonstration programs and related technology (Perehnia and Allen, 1995).

Despite the relatively low capital and operational costs and the potential benefits in improving access to primary care and preventive screening, the adoption of MHCs and telemedicine remained low among American hospitals between 2008 and 2017. Based on the AHA annual survey database, only about 25 percent of the hospitals adopted telemedicine in 2017. The rate of adoption for MHCs was only 9 percent in 2008, with almost a flat growth curve, the MHC adoption rate only increased to 12 percent in 2017.

What factors contribute to the adoption of MHCs and telemedicine? Can inter-hospital dynamics such as competition, collaboration, and coopetition account for the variation of adoption of the two new models of primary care service delivery? Table 5 presents four logistic regression models that answer these questions. In Table 5, Models (1) and (2) present two panel logistic regression models for the variable measuring the adoption of mobile health services. Column (2) is the panel logistic regression model with year-fixed effects and the interaction between competition and collaboration for the variable measuring the adoption of mobile health care. In this model, competition has a positive and statistically significant coefficient ($b = 0.343$, $p < 0.01$), and the interaction term "Competition X collaboration" has a negative and statistically significant coefficient ($b = -0.702$, $p < 0.01$). The statistical results mean that inter-hospital collaboration moderates the effect of competition on the adoption of mobile health care.

Column (4) is the full model for the adoption of telemedicine. The AHA only started to surveying hospitals about their adoption of telemedicine in 2017. Therefore, this model is estimated based only on cross-section data in 2017. In column (4), the coefficient for "Competition X collaboration" is negative and statistically significant ($b = -1.035$, $p < 0.01$), which is consistent with findings in column (2). Substantively, this negative interaction term means that competition and collaboration do not operate as two opposing and separated factors in affecting the adoption of telemedicine. The adoption of this new model of service delivery is driven by the interplay between competition and collaboration.

Different from findings regarding technology innovation, in these two cases of service innovation, competition, and collaboration appear to be counterbalancing forces for innovation adoption. Figure 6 facilitates the assessment of how the adoption of mobile health care and telemedicine varies along with inter-hospital collaboration in the scenarios of low and high market competition. The left panel visualizes the case of adopting mobile health care. Market competition exhibits a positive association with the probability of adoption, but only when inter-hospital collaborative ties are weak, and there is a low intensity of using collaboration for service delivery. The effect size of market competition, furthermore, is quite small. For isolated hospitals that do not rely on collaborative alliance for service delivery, the predicted probability of adopting mobile health care is around 0.08, which increased to 0.1 when silo hospitals face high market competition.

Table 5 Coopetition and service innovation in American hospitals, 2008–2017: Logistic regression models

VARIABLES	(1) Mobile health care	(2) Mobile health care	(3) Telemedicine	(4) Telemedicine
Competition	0.173***	0.343***	−0.074	0.157
	(0.054)	(0.075)	(0.132)	(0.166)
Collaboration	−0.473***	−0.176	0.224	0.554**
	(0.084)	(0.124)	(0.174)	(0.226)
Competition X collaboration	—	−0.702***	—	−1.035**
		(0.221)		(0.464)
Public	1.278***	1.281***	0.732***	0.755***
	(0.078)	(0.079)	(0.157)	(0.159)
Nonprofit	1.347***	1.353***	0.838***	0.863***
	(0.074)	(0.074)	(0.148)	(0.150)
General	0.906***	0.911***	0.703***	0.716***
	(0.076)	(0.076)	(0.148)	(0.148)
Rural	−0.385***	−0.370***	0.215**	0.234**
	(0.049)	(0.050)	(0.104)	(0.104)
Medical school	−0.245***	−0.244***	−0.595***	−0.598***
	(0.040)	(0.040)	(0.096)	(0.096)

Table 5 (cont.)

VARIABLES	(1) Mobile health care	(2) Mobile health care	(3) Telemedicine	(4) Telemedicine
Bed Capacity	0.289***	0.289***	−0.079**	−0.078**
	(0.014)	(0.013)	(0.033)	(0.033)
FTE	0.000***	0.000***	0.000***	0.000***
	(0.000)	(0.000)	(0.000)	(0.000)
Constant	−5.102***	−5.179***	−1.538***	−1.633***
	(0.150)	(0.153)	(0.270)	(0.276)
Year-Fixed effects	Yes	Yes	No	No
Observations	46,120	46,120	4,288	4,288

Robust standard errors in parentheses.

*** p < 0.01, ** p < 0.05, * p < 0.1

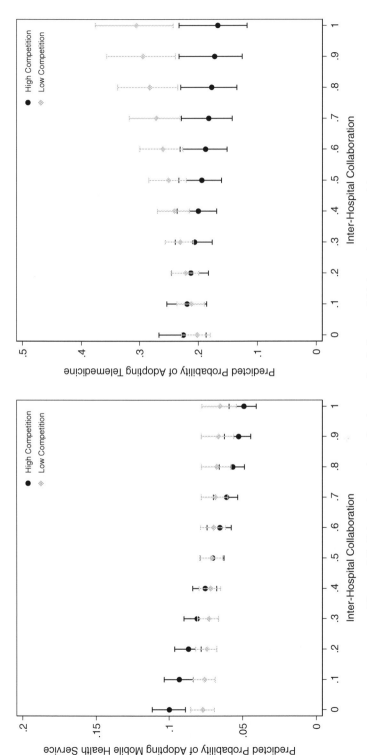

Figure 6 Collaboration and service innovation in low and high market competition

The right panel in Figure 6 shows the case of adopting telemedicine, in which there is no conclusive evidence that market competition alone drives up the adoption. Inter-hospital collaboration, however, is found to be positively associated with adoption in the scenario of low market competition. High collaboration, coupled with low competition, is associated with a mean probability of 0.3 to adopt telemedicine. When market competition is high, the probability of adopting telemedicine decreases to approximately 0.2 among highly networked hospitals.

Why has the adoption of mobile health care and telemedicine remained so low in the scenario of coopetition? Mobile health care and telemedicine are service innovations that primarily focus on expanding primary care service. Both would help hospitals to expand the outreach to patients. In the case of adopting mobile health clinics, hospitals are likely to increase the total outputs of primary care services from reaching out to vulnerable and economically disadvantaged communities. Primary care service, however, does not guarantee improved operating margins and profitability of service. Compared with technology-intensive services areas, primary care is suboptimal for revenue generation. Figure 7 shows patterns of innovation adoption that are in sharp comparison with findings regarding coopetition and technology innovation.

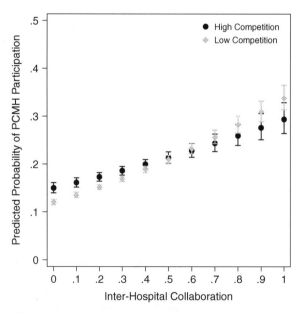

Figure 7 Collaboration and pioneers of patient-centered care in low and high market competition

One possible explanation is that coopetition brings both competitive pressures on improving revenue and networked channels for speedy transfer of knowledge and experiences regarding innovation. High market competition could possibly drive hospitals toward technology-intensive service areas, which are reimbursed better than primary care services (Chandra, 2012). Previous studies also suggest hospitals with great financial constraints are more likely to give priority to innovations and strategies that help them to expand the reach to well-insured patients rather than serving the low-income communities (Carrier et al., 2012). Findings in this section suggest that the "invisible hand" of the market might not always be the best route for spurring innovation. Collaborative service innovation might occur in low-profitable service areas, but only when service organizations face low competitive pressures from the market.

5 Pioneers of Patient-Centered Care

In the previous sections, I analyzed the adoption of new medical technology and new methods of service delivery that target patient outreach. In this section, two additional innovation activities are examined in the area of patient-centered care provision – the adoption of the patient-centered medical home (PCMH) model and hospitals' participation in accountable care organizations (ACOs). PCMH and ACOs can also be viewed as institutional innovation, in that they introduce new ways of coordinating health care services.

Traditionally, in the US fee-for-service system, various hospital care services are provided to patients based on the pay-as-you-go model. Primary care, compared with hospitalization care, has long remained a peripheral service area in the hospital sector. Aiming at providing affordability of care and establishing a primary care basis for improving the value of care for patients, patient-centered medical home was created as a new model of coordinated service delivery. PCMH has also been deemed a means of transforming and reforming the US health care system. The medical home model of primary care delivery centers on the provision of comprehensive primary care services through coordinated communication shared decision-making between patients, care providers, and patients' families.

The first nationwide PCMH demonstration program was launched in 2006 by the American Academy of Family Physicians with different family practices (Nutting et al., 2011). Although the initial pilot project was trialed among individual family physicians, not hospital organizations, the hospital industry has begun to catch up during the past few years as PCMH showed promise in improving the quality of primary care, increasing primary care utilization and helping hospitals to reduce costs associated with readmission after hospital discharges (DeVries et al., 2012; Paustain et al., 2013). Many public safety-net hospitals and urban hospitals in the nonprofit sector also welcome the potential benefits of improved primary care through PCMH programs, because improved accessibility, affordability, and quality of care would reduce unnecessary and costly emergency room visits. Although both are aimed at improving primary care provision, the PCMH model differs substantially from the use of mobile health clinics and telemedicine. The adoption of PCMH will require a reorganization of the care delivery process and lead to the creation of new organizational forms, while the use of mobile health clinics and telemedicine does not lead to large-scale changes in how care is coordinated for patients.

After the ACA was enacted, PCMH was viewed as an integral part of health care reform for improving the quality and outcomes of health care. The concept of patient-centered care provision was also transplanted into the new payment model, accountable care organizations (ACOs), under the ACA. Pilot ACO programs were tested between 2005 and 2010. After the enactment of the ACA, Medicare introduced its pioneer ACO program in 2012. After the full rollout of the ACA in 2014, hospitals' participation in ACOs began to increase substantially. Similar to PCMH, ACOs bring together primary care providers, behavioral health, and other health care professionals to create a more individualized patient-centered care process. While PCMH focuses on the provision of primary care services, ACOs bring patients a broader spectrum of services and reduce unnecessary duplication in care through coordination.

Table 6 shows how the adoption of PCMH and ACO participation in American hospitals changed between 2011 and 2017. Because the adoption of PCMH in hospitals occurred after 2010, the AHA started to survey its member hospitals about PCMH adoption in 2011. For the case of ACOs, AHA only began to collect data on ACO participation in 2016. In 2011, about 14.5 percent of hospitals adopted PCMH, but within seven years, PCMH diffused among hospitals at a robust pace. In 2017, over 45 percent of hospitals adopted patient-centered medical home programs. The year 2017 saw a substantial jump in adoption rates across all three sectors. It is also worth noting that the adoption of PCMH in the private for-profit sector had remained dormant until very recently.

As for ACO participation, nonprofit hospitals are leaders in this particular health care innovation. In 2016, near 45 percent of nonprofit hospitals participated in ACOs, and public hospitals had a noticeably lower participation rate of 18.5 percent. The private sector has the lowest ACO participation rate. In 2016, only about one-tenth of private hospitals participated in ACOs. Growth in ACO participation was also uneven across the three sectors. From 2016 to 2017, ACO participation increased by 7 percent in the nonprofit sector, 3 percent in the

Table 6 Trends in adopting PCMHs and ACOs in American hospitals, 2011–2017

Year	PCMHs				ACOs			
	Overall	Public	Nonprofit	Private	Total	Public	Nonprofit	Private
2011	14.5%	12.9%	19.1%	2.4%				
2012	16.5%	15.0%	22.1%	2.5%				
2013	20.2%	18.0%	26.9%	3.5%				
2014	22.8%	21.0%	30.1%	3.8%				
2015	23.5%	21.8%	31.5%	3.4%				
2016	25.5%	23.5%	34.0%	4.2%	32.6%	18.5%	45.7%	10.5%
2017	45.7%	66.6%	41.8%	40%	38.6%	21.5%	52.7%	12.6%

Data source: American Hospital Association Annual Hospital Survey Database.

public sector, and 2 percent in the for-profit sector. Overall, nonprofit hospitals are pioneers in moving toward patient-centered care provision. Private for-profit hospitals lag behind both public and nonprofit hospitals in providing patient-centered care.

Can the coopetition framework explain PCMH adoption and ACO participation? In Table 7, I presented additional logistic regression models that link competition, collaboration, and coopetition to hospitals' adoption of PCMH and ACO participation. Due to availability of data, models for PCMH adoption are based on data from 2011 to 2017. Models for ACO participation are based on data from only 2016 and 2017. As for ACO participation, the AHA not only surveyed all its member hospitals about their participation in ACO, but also asked a random subsample of hospitals if ACO were established for Medicaid patients.

For the adoption of PCMH and Medicaid ACO, Table 7 shows that the variable competition always has a positive and statistically significant coefficient. Collaboration also has a positive association with the adoption of PCMH and ACO participation. Looking at the interaction term "Competition X collaboration," Models (2), (4), and (6) consistently produce negative and statistically significant coefficients, meaning that the interplay between competition and collaboration also significantly affects PCMH adoption and ACO participation.

Because the coefficients of the interaction term are consistent across Models (2), (4), and (6), for the sake of simplicity, I use Figure 7 to illustrate how competition and collaboration jointly shape the adoption of patient-centered care via the PCMH model. Figure 7 plots the predicted probability of adopting the PCMH model of primary care delivery across the full range of the variable for inter-hospital collaboration in different scenarios of market competition.

In both market competition scenarios, inter-hospital collaboration is always positively associated with the adoption of PCMH. Hospitals that are embedded in collaborative service delivery networks are much more likely to adopt the PCMH model compared with isolated monopoly and silo hospitals in neck-to-neck competition. The effect size of inter-hospital collaboration is also large. In the absence of inter-hospital collaboration, the probability of adopting PCMH is around 0.1 in a scenario of low competition and 0.15 in a scenario of high competition. In both scenarios, the probability of adopting PCMH increases substantially as inter-hospital collaboration grows. When collaboration is the highest, the predicted probability of adopting PCMH is around 0.3.

Both Table 7 and Figure 7 also show that market competition does have a positive impact on the adoption of PCMH, but only so when there is an absence of collaborative service provision. The effect size of competition on adopting PCMH, moreover, is very small and negligible, compared with the effect size of collaboration.

Table 7 Competition, collaboration, and participation in patient-centered medical home programs and the accountable care organizations

VARIABLES	(1) Medical home program	(2) Medical home program	(3) ACO	(4) ACO	(5) ACO for Medicaid patients	(6) ACO for Medicaid patients
Competition	0.146***	0.335***	-0.148	-0.060	0.303**	1.080***
	(0.056)	(0.081)	(0.092)	(0.144)	(0.141)	(0.242)
Collaboration	1.163***	1.373***	2.503***	2.584***	-0.046	0.606**
	(0.077)	(0.102)	(0.124)	(0.162)	(0.195)	(0.254)
Competition X collaboration	–	-0.608***	–	-2.663***	–	-2.015***
		(0.201)		(0.335)		(0.499)
Public hospital	1.524***	1.530***	0.255**	0.259**	-0.631***	-0.586***
	(0.080)	(0.080)	(0.108)	(0.108)	(0.212)	(0.214)
Nonprofit hospital	1.545***	1.555***	1.219***	1.224***	-0.354**	-0.311*
	(0.075)	(0.075)	(0.092)	(0.093)	(0.170)	(0.173)
General hospital	1.237***	1.234***	1.611***	1.604***	-0.135	-0.184
	(0.072)	(0.072)	(0.099)	(0.099)	(0.195)	(0.196)
Rural hospital	-0.295***	-0.284***	-0.281***	-0.276***	-0.092	-0.051
	(0.044)	(0.044)	(0.070)	(0.070)	(0.126)	(0.127)

Table 7 (cont.)

	(1)	(2)	(3)	(4)	(5)	(6)
Medical school	-0.523***	-0.522***	-0.093	-0.092	-0.124	-0.128
	(0.040)	(0.040)	(0.067)	(0.067)	(0.103)	(0.104)
Bed capacity	0.041***	0.041***	0.059***	0.059***	-0.073**	-0.084***
	(0.015)	(0.015)	(0.023)	(0.023)	(0.032)	(0.032)
FTE	0.000***	0.000***	0.000***	0.000***	0.000	0.000
	(0.000)	(0.000)	(0.000)	(0.000)	(0.000)	(0.000)
Constant	-4.081***	-4.144***	-3.769***	-3.792***	-0.226	-0.416
	(0.149)	(0.151)	(0.200)	(0.202)	(0.341)	(0.349)
Year-fixed effects	Yes	Yes	Yes	Yes	Yes	Yes
observations	27,006	27,006	8,293	8,293	2,918	2,918

Robust standard errors in parentheses.

*** p < 0.01, ** p < 0.05, * p < 0.1

What about the coopetition thesis? Figure 7 shows some evidence supporting the coopetition argument. In a scenario of high market competition, the adoption rate is much higher when inter-hospital collaboration is also high than when collaboration is low. Considering competition and collaboration together, the lowest probability of adoption is observed among hospitals that are isolated monopolies. They do not engage in collaborative service provision, neither do they face high market competition. Compare the adoption rates under coopetition and just high market competition, Figure 7 shows that the probability of adopting PCMH is substantially higher under coopetition than that under the neck-to-neck competition. Analyzing service innovation that involves fundamental changes in how health care is coordinated, I find the dual logics of collaborative innovation and coopetition.

6 Concluding Discussions: Collaborative Innovation in Competitive Markets

In this Element, I connect the literature on innovation and theories of inter-organizational dynamics to explain what factors drive frontline service organizations' innovation. Different from the previous small-N network studies (Raab, Lemaire, and Proven, 2013), this Element uses a large-N national longitudinal sample of organizations (American hospitals), and measures coopetition based on objective measures of market competition and interorganizational collaboration. Analyzing the joint effect of inter-hospital collaboration and external market competition, I found robust evidence that shows that networking and collaboration influence organizational innovation both directly and indirectly. Using different empirical indicators of innovation, I found complex ways by which competition, collaboration, and coopetition are linked to innovation. The complexity of how interorganizational dynamics drive innovation mirror findings in previous studies in the context of service innovation in local governments. As Walker (2014) synthesizes from the voluminous literature on public service innovation, public sector innovation is driven by a complex array of internal and external factors, and the links between these antecedents vary by the types and characteristics of innovation activity.

A more careful comparison of empirical findings in this Element leads to several important conclusions drawn from the following synopsis of results based on innovation type and inter-hospital relationships. These thematic conclusions may inform future theory building regarding the relational foundations of public service innovation. Findings in this research also shed light on important practical implications for managing innovation in complex interorganizational relationships.

6.1 Neither Competition Nor Collaboration Alone Drives Innovation

The effect of market competition on innovation has been a longstanding theme in the literature on private sector innovation. The idea that competition spurs change has proliferated in the public and nonprofit management literature since the New Public Management movement. Findings in this research challenge the conventional wisdom that market competition is the best route to allocate new ideas and new technology. The empirical analysis of this research covers various forms of innovation activities in the US mixed-ownership health care system. Tracing more than 4,000 US hospitals in a ten-year time period, this research finds very limited evidence that competition alone drives up innovation.

To systematically gauge the key empirical findings, I took a configurational approach (Raab, Lemaire, and Proven, 2013) to compare findings regarding different types of innovation, cost, and uncertainty associated with the adoption of each specific innovation, and different interorganizational dynamics. In Table 8, configurational analysis allows a comparative assessment of innovation across the conditions of competition, collaboration, and coopetition, while taking into account different innovation characteristics.

Table 8 shows, across the seven innovation adoption activities, that market competition alone does not accelerate the adoption of innovation. In cases wherein a positive association between inter-hospital competition and innovation adoption is observed, such as the adoption of EHRs and PCMHs, the effect size of competition is found to be very small. In most cases, the probabilities of innovation adoption are comparable among monopolist hospitals and those in a crowded market with neck-to-neck competition. Hospital innovation remains low on these two opposing ends of the market competition spectrum. This pattern aligns with recent research that suggests a non-monotonic inverted-U relationship between competition and innovation (Aghion et al., 2005).

Why is the active adoption of technology and service innovation absent in neck-to-neck competition? In highly competitive markets, barriers to innovation adoption vary across different innovation types. Medical technologies, such as medical robots and electronic health records, are associated with high capital and operating costs. High market competition is likely to lead to reduced market share and to add increased financial constraints on hospitals. The high front-end costs might prevent hospitals, particularly those that are small and medium in size, and those that experience financial distress, from acquiring expensive new medical technology. Competitors in a crowded local service market not only provide substitutable services, but also compete for human capital from the same talent pool. Pressures of recruiting and retaining specialized health care technicians and

Table 8 Summary of key findings by innovation type

Innovation type	Technology innovation	Organization process innovation	Service innovation
Cases	1 Robotic surgery 2 Virtual reality technology 3 Electronic health record	1 PCMH 2 ACO	1 Mobile health clinics (MHC) 2 Telemedicine
Innovation characteristics			
Capital cost	High	Low	Low
Operating cost	High	Moderate	Low
Uncertainty in profitability and revenue impact	Low Ample evidence on revenue increase	Low Evidence on cost saving	HighLack of evidence on revenue impact
Visibility	High	Moderate	Low, only with targeted patients
Effects of interorganizational dynamics			
Competition	Does not drive innovation up, in the case of EHRs, there is a small chilling effect	No salient impact Some positive statistical association, but negligible effect size	Very small positive effects when collaboration is low
Collaboration	Some positive effects in the case of VR technology	Some positive effects	Positive effects when market competition is low

Table 8 (cont.)

Innovation type	Technology innovation	Organization process innovation	Service innovation
Coopetition	Large positive effects, accelerating innovation in competitive markets	Large positive effects, accelerating innovation in competitive markets	No clear evidence, competition and collaboration have counterbalancing influences

professionals also can increase along with the neck-to-neck competition. Human capital might become another barrier for adopting new medical technology when hospitals face zero-sum market competition.

Another paradoxical finding regarding competition and innovation is that the adoption of customer-oriented service innovation does not go hand in hand with increases in inter-hospital competition. Hospitals facing increasing pressure from competitive market environments have but a small market share in their local service area. In such a setting, no consistent evidence is observed that greater efforts are devoted to patient-centered service innovation activities. These empirical findings clearly show that health care innovation in the USA cannot be explained simply by market competition logic.

The second conclusion drawn from this research is that the theme of collaborative innovation finds some evidence, but that collaboration alone cannot fully explain health care innovation. The panel study on American hospitals during the past decade uncovers inter-hospital collaboration as an external determinant of innovation across numerous innovation areas. Compared with hospitals that primarily produce in-house health services, hospitals that participate in collaborative service networks are more likely to provide mobile health services, more likely to adopt new medical technology, and more likely to be leaders of patient-centered health care. These findings are consistent with theories and empirical studies that claim collaborative relationships within service networks facilitate the spread of new technology and new methods of service delivery (Huang, 2014; Provan et al., 2013). They confirm the theme in the collaboration literature that interorganizational ties can facilitate innovation efforts and are important relational foundations of organizational change (O'Toole, 1997; Robinson, 2006). Yet the theme of collaborative innovation is accompanied by several caveats. Across the seven innovation activities, the adoption of virtual reality technology and patient-centered care increases as inter-hospital collaboration grows, regardless of the level of competition. This pattern is not observed for the adoption of medical robots and EHRs. For low-cost low-visibility innovation such as mobile health clinics, inter-hospital collaboration has a positive effect on innovation adoption only when market competition is low.

6.2 Coopetition as the Alternative Path for Innovation

Key results regarding the interactive effects between collaboration and competition shows more nuances about health care innovation in the US health care sector. These findings suggest that service organizations' innovation activities may be driven by a complex set of external factors including both market constraints and their relationships with partner organizations. This more complex view of innovation links theoretical insights from both the NPM approach and the collaboration approach and offers more nuances into how coopetition represents different interorganizational dynamics from neck-to-neck competition and sheer collaboration.

As for the adoption of new medical technology and patient-centered care models, there is clear evidence that coopetition has greater positive effects on innovation than competition and collaboration alone. Across six out of the seven innovation indicators (apart from the adoption of VR technology), monopolist hospitals are always the laggards of innovation adoption. Conversely, hospitals that simultaneously face high market competition and inter-hospital collaboration are always the leaders of adopting new technology and high-visibility reforms of patient-centered care. Coopetition is also found to be different from collaboration. Although both can promote innovation adoption, coopetition exhibits greater positive effects than collaboration in accelerating innovation. These findings confirm the theoretical proposition suggested by Lado et al. (1997), that is, that interactions between organizations under coopetition are not a zero-sum game. Coopetition produces positive-sum interactions and lead to the creation of "syncretic" efforts.

As Table 8 highlights, key empirical findings on coopetition are also indicative of potential decision tradeoffs between different innovation activities. While organizations can consider both service and technology innovation, different innovation tasks come with varying levels of task difficulty and cost structures. For example, technology innovation involving medical robots come with high fixed cost for initial installation and high varying cost of equipment maintenance. But such high-cost technology innovation is often associated with greater certainty about the returns (e.g., increased profit margin by providing robot-assisted surgery) and maintains a high-visibility among peer hospitals, physicians, and patients. Similarly, transforming traditional pay-as-you-go health care services into the patient-centered medical home model or the accountable care organization model introduces high-cost large-scale changes that also show high visibility. For low-cost innovation such as the adoption of mobile health clinics, the analysis does not yield conclusive evidence about the role of coopetition. It appears that coopetition might make organizations prioritize on high-visibility innovation activities.

6.3 Practical Implications

Several important practical implications can be drawn from this Element, regarding the use of competitive mechanism and networking strategies to promote change and innovation. Inspired by the New Public Management movement, health care in the USA and many other developed countries has confronted with increasing needs in innovation to improving service quality while reducing costs. In the past decade, the national health care reform under the ACA has introduced many pro-competition changes to the hospital sector. For instance, CMS's new hospital quality star rating system adds competition among hospitals for both reputation and Medicare funding resources. Even in the public and nonprofit sectors, hospitals are incentivized to engage in "medical arms race" in adding more high-tech services (Trinh et al., 2008). European countries, such as the Netherlands and the United Kingdom, have experienced similar trends of introducing pro-competition reforms to their health care systems (van den Broek et al., 2014). Using market-based mechanisms to promote the efficiency and quality of public services has also become a common practice in other public service sectors beyond health care (Whitford, 2007). Findings in this research highlight the possibility that pro-competition reforms might not always effectively achieving the goal of promoting change and innovation in the health care sector. New policies that do not consider the dual logic of competition and collaboration may fail to deliver.

This research finds coopetition as a viable path for innovation in highly competitive environments. When hospitals are constrained by fierce market competition, forming a horizontal alliance with peer hospitals and competitors might help to reduce the zero-sum neck-to-neck competition. Coopetition, however, is not evenly seen in the public, nonprofit, and private sectors. In the US context, a large share of public hospitals faces competition, as they monopolize their local service markets. Competitive pressures are the highest among for-profit hospitals, and coopetition is mostly seen among nonprofit hospitals. This complex picture offers some practical insights on how to map the coopetition strategy to different institutional contexts. Public hospitals, such as federally owned VA hospitals and safety-net hospitals owned by local health districts, could lack the steam of change and innovation, because they do not face competition in their local service area. Too much neck-to-neck competition among private for-profits, on the contrary, might drive for-profit hospitals toward high-profit margin service areas and keep them away from innovations that will improve patient experiences and community-based health care. In both situations, developing coopetition through cross-sector collaboration may reduce barriers to innovation and service improvement. Coopetition networks that go beyond a local market boundary may also help to promote innovation.

6.4 Concluding Thoughts on Future Research Agenda

Using the American health care context, I show that the coopetition framework is a fruitful approach to examine inter-organizational relationships and organizational behavior. While public management research in the past two decades primarily focuses on how the formation and consequences of collaborative networks, this Element adds to the literature by showing that inter-organizational networks can have both direct and indirect impacts on organizational behavior such as innovation. It complements the theoretical approach that focuses on internal organizational factors by conceptualizing inter-organizational dynamics as an important dimension of the external social environment of organizations. Research on coopetition, nonetheless, still remains to be sparse and under-developed in the public and nonprofit management literature. Future research needs to be developed to advance theory building and the cumulation of evidence regarding the formation and consequences of coopetition.

First, the conceptualization of coopetition can be expanded from horizontal inter-organizational relationships to account for the multiplexity of collaborative networks and coopetition relationships. Theories of social networks suggest as networks grow in size and complexity of resource composition, network structures will also evolve (Milward and Provan, 1998). As such, both competition and collaboration may occur vertically cross different units within a network and/or across different vertical layers of networks. Empirical measures of coopetition can be improved and extended by examining both horizontal and vertical relationships across organizations. The concept of coopetition can also be applied to measure relationships between different networks (Tsai, 2002). One may track different types of collaboration among competitors instead of just focusing on the overall intensity of coopetition. For example, Agranoff and McGuire (2003) point out that collaborative networks and relationships are driven by a complex array of motivations; thus, they can be divided into four categories: information networks, capacity-building networks, outreach networks, and action networks. How these different motivations are managed in coopetition alliances remains to be explored.

Second, the dual presence of competition and collaboration naturally implies possible tensions within collaborative relationships. Existing theoretical work on coopetition and qualitative case studies suggest coopetition can increase value and produce social capital among organizations but may also require balancing the possible tension between competition and collaboration (Bengtsson and Kock, 2014). How organizations reconcile the potential tension between competition and collaboration makes an important future research agenda. Coopetition often rises from collaborative networks that primarily connect similar service providers in the same service sector (e.g., hospital networks, business alliances in the same service industry). The empirical analysis of inter-hospital collaboration primarily focuses on hospitals' formal partnerships with peer hospitals. Beyond peer-to-peer relationships, organizations can also be embedded in other collaborative relationships within their broad local communities and participate in multi-sector networks (Hogg and Varda, 2016). Inter-organizational collaboration, moreover, can exist through both formal and informal ties. Future research can extend the coopetition agenda by comparing the influence of peer-to-peer coopetition relationships relative to other types of community-based network, as well as assessing the potential differences between formal and informal partnerships.

Third, this Element explores organizational-level innovation adoption as an outcome of coopetition. Empirical measures of innovation adoption as discrete choices lead to parsimonious statistical models on coopetition and innovation. But this approach might overlook innovation decisions as portfolio choices and the potential trade-offs between different types of innovation. Though being a rare phenomenon, a small proportion of US hospitals also cut back from using new medical technology and new modes of service provision after the initial adoption. With longitudinal data, it is possible to conceptualize and model innovation activities as repeatable events based on portfolio choices. The coopetition framework can also be applied to exploring if decisions in cutting back on certain innovation activities are tied to the dual institutional forces of competition and collaboration.

Fourth, the coopetition theoretical framework offers a new lens to further explore how organizational factors and leadership characteristics might linked to the external inter-organizational dynamics in shaping innovation. Because the varying size, skill assets, and internal structures, service organizations could involve in different coopetition relationships with their peers. At the aggregate level, these organizational characteristics can also affect the skill and resource composition of networks of coopetition. Top-level leaders, due to their different personal characteristics and leadership styles, may also manage the coopetition relationship differently (Damanpour and Schneider, 2006). Probing how these internal factors interact with the relational foundations of innovation remains will be a natural extension to this research.

While empirically showing the link between coopetition and innovation, this Element also raises several future research questions regarding how public and nonprofit managers may effectively use coopetition strategies for promoting innovation and improving performance. First, it is imperative for future research in this area to assess whether early or late uptake of innovation will produce differential effects on organizational performance. While leaders in innovation might enjoy comparative advantage brought by early adoption of new technology, new service process, and new organizational forms, they may also face high uncertainty regarding whether innovation can produce desired performance improvement. It is conceivable that coopetition in networks can become effective channels for learning and optimizing innovation decisions. As Nembhard, Cheruan, and Bradley (2014) argue, innovation can be implemented by internal creative problem solving and by importing peers' best practices through learning and imitation. The coopetition framework introduced in this Element offers a plausible approach to further explore the interplay between these different mechanisms of innovation.

Last but not least, in the era of information technology, public and nonprofit organizations are facing rapid and constant changes in their external environment, consequently, they need effective strategies for making adaptive decision making. Many public services sectors may experience external shocks such as the great recession and the current Covid-19 pandemic, a natural extension to this Element is to explore how coopetition strategies might be used for improving organizational learning and resilience to system shocks.

References

Aghion, P., N. Bloom, R. Blundell, R. Griffith, & P. Howitt (2005). "Competition and Innovation: An Inverted-U Relationship." *Quarterly Journal of Economics*, 120 (2): 701–28.

Aghion, P., P. Howitt, & S. Prantl (2013). "Revising the Relationship between Competition, Patenting, and Innovation." In *Advances in Economics and Econometrics*, eds. Aaron Acemoglu, Manuel Arellano, & Eddie Dekel. New York, NY: Cambridge University Press, pp. 451–55.

Agranoff, R. (2008). "Enhancing Performance through Public Sector Networks: Mobilizing Human Capital in Communities of Practice." *Public Performance & Management Review*, 31(3): 320–47.

Agranoff, R.. & M. McGuire (1999). "Managing in Network Settings." *Public Administration Review*, 16(1): 18–41.

Agranoff, R. & M. McGuire (2003). *Collaborative Public Management: New Strategies for Local Governments*. Washington, DC: Georgetown University Press.

Akkerman, A. & R. Torenvlied (2011). "Managing the Environment: Effects of Network Ambition on Agency Performance." *Public Management Review*, 13(1): 159–74.

Aldrich, Haward E. & M. Ruff (2006). *Organizations Evolving*, 2nd ed. Thousand Oaks, CA: Sage Publications.

Amirkhanyan, A. (2008). "Privatizing Public Nursing Homes: Examining the Effects on Quality and Access." *Public Administration Review*, 68(4): 665–80.

Ansell, C. & A. Gash (2008). "Collaborative Governance in Theory and Practice". *Journal of Public Administration Research and Theory*, 18(4): 543–71.

Baer, M. (2010). "The Strength-of-Weak-Ties Perspective on Creativity. A Comprehensive Examination and Extension." *Journal of Applied Psychology*, 95(3): 592–601.

Baker, L.C. (2001.) "Measuring Competition in Health Care Markets." *Health Service Research*, 36(1): 223–51.

Balas, E.A. & W.W. Chapman (2018). "The Roadmap for Diffusion of Innovation in Health Care." *Health Affairs*, 37(2): 198–204.

Balla, S. (2001). "Interstate Professional Associations and the Diffusion of Policy Innovations." *American Politics Research*, 29(2): 221–45.

Barretta, A. (2008). "The Functioning of Co-opetition in the Health Care Sector: An Explorative Analysis." *Scandinavian Journal of Management*, 24(3): 209.

Barrutia, J.M. & C. Echebarria (2018). "Drivers of Exploitative and Explorative Innovation in a Collaborative Public-Sector Context." *Public Management Review*, 21(3): 446–72.

Bazzoli, G.J., S.M. Shortell, N.L. Dubbs, C. Chan, & P. Kralovec (1999). "A Taxonomy of Health Networks and Systems Bringing Order Out of Chaos." *Health Services Research*, 33(6): 1683–717.

Beck, N., J.N. Katz, & R. Tucker (1998). "Taking Time Seriously: Time-Series-Cross-Section Analysis with a Binary Dependent Variable." *American Journal of Political Science*, 42(4): 1260–88.

Bengtsson, M. & S. Kock (2014). "Coopetition – Quo Vadis? Past Accomplishments and Future Challenges." *Industrial Management Research*, 42(2): 180–8.

Bennett, C. & M. Howlett (1992). "The Lessons of Learning: Reconciling Theories of Policy Learning and Policy Change." *Policy Sciences*, 25(3): 275–94.

Bennett, R.A.. & R. Kottasz (2011). "Strategic, Competitive, and Cooperative Approaches to Internationalisation in European Business Schools." *Journal of Marketing Management*, 27(11–12): 1087–116.

Berardo, R. (2009). "Processing Complexity in Networks: A Study of Informal Collaboration and its Effect on Organizational Success." *Policy Studies Journal*, 37(3): 521–39.

Berry, F.S., R.S. Brower, S.O. Choi et al. (2004). "Three Traditions of Network Research: What the Public Management Research Agenda Can Learn from Other Research Communities." *Public Administration Review*, 64(5): 539–52.

Blute, M.L. & A.L. Presdipino (2014). "Factors Associated with Adoption of Robotic Surgical Technology in US Hospitals and Relationship to Radical Prostatectomy Procedure Volume." *Annuals of Surgery*, 259(1): 7–9.

Bouwen, R. & R. Fry (1991). "Organizational Innovation and Learning: Four Patterns of Dialog between the Dominant Logic and the New Logic." *Industrial Studies of Management and Organizations*, 21(4): 37–51.

Boyne, G. & K.J. Meier (2009). "Environmental Turbulence, Organizational Stability, and Public Service Performance." *Administration and Society*, 40 (8): 799–824.

Bozeman, B. (2000). "Technology Transfer and Public Policy: A Review of Research and Theory." *Research Policy*, 29: 627–55.

Brandenburger, A.M. & B.J. Nalebuff (1997). "Co-opetition: Competitive and Cooperative Business Strategies for the Digital Economy." *Strategy & Leadership*, 25(6): 28–33.

Brown, L. & S. Osborne (2013). "Risk and Innovation: Towards a Framework for Risk Governance in Public Services." *Public Management Review*, 15(2): 186–208.

Bunger, A., M.S. Choi, H. McDowell, & T. Gregoire (2020). "Competition among Mental Health Organizations: Environmental Drivers and Strategic Responses." *Administration and Policy in Mental Health and Mental Health Service Research*, forthcoming.

Burt, R.S. (2004). "Structural Holes and Good Ideas." *American Journal of Sociology*, 110(2): 349–99.

Carrier E.R, M. Dowling, & R.A. Berenson (2012). "Hospitals' Expansion in Quest of Well-Insured Patients: Will the Outcome Be Better Care, More Cost, or Both?" *Health Affairs*, 31(4): 827–35.

Carter, D.B. & C.S. Signorino (2010). "Back to the Future: Modeling Time Dependence in Binary Data." *Political Analysis*, 18(3): 271–92.

Cassel, B.J., B. Brown, M. Roggers et al. (2018). "Palliative Care Leadership Centers Are Key to the Diffusion of Palliative Care Innovation." *Health Affairs*, 37(2): 231–9.

Chandra, A. & J. Skinner (2012). "Technology Growth and Expenditure Growth in Health Care." *Journal of Economic Literature*, 50 (3): 645–80.

Chen, J. & R.M. Walker (2019). "Public Service Innovation: A Typology." *Public Management Review*, forthcoming.

Chen, W.R. (2008). "Determinants of Firm's Backward and Forward-Looking R& D Research Behavior." *Organization Science*, 19(4): 609–22.

Damanpour, F. & M. Schneider (2006). "Phases of the Adoption of Innovation in Organizations: Effects of Environment, Organization and Top Managers." *British Journal of Management*, 17(3): 215–36.

Damanpour, F. & M. Schneider (2009). "Characteristics of Innovation and Innovation Adoption in Public Organizations: Assessing the Role of Managers." *Journal of Public Administration Research and Theory*, 19 (4): 495–522.

De Lancer Julnes, P. & E. Gibson (2016). "*Innovation in the Public and Nonprofit Sectors.*" New York, NY: Routledge.

Devece, C., D.E. Riberio-Soriano, & D. Palacios-Marqués (2019). "Coopetition as the New Trend in Inter-Firm Alliances: Literature Review and Research Patterns." *Review of Managerial Science*, 13 (2): 207–26.

DeVries, A., C.H. Li, G. Sridhar et al. (2012). "Impact of Medical Homes on Quality, Healthcare Utilization, and Costs." *American Journal of Managed Care*, 18(9): 534–44.

DiMaggio, P.J. & W.W. Powell (1983). "The Iron Cage Revisited: Institutional Isomorphism and Collective Rationality in Organizational Fields." *American Sociological Review*, 48(2): 147–60.

Dyer, J.H. &H. Singh (1998)."The Relational View: Coopetition Strategy and Sources of Inter-Organizational Competitive Advantage." *Academy of Management Review*, 23(4):660–79.

Edgerley L.P., Y.Y. El-Sayed, M.L. Druzin, M. Kiernan, & K.I. Daniels (2007). "Use of A Community Mobile Health Van to Increase Early Access to Prenatal Care." *Maternal Child Health Journal*, 11(3): 235–9.

Ekeland, A.G., A. Bowes, & S. Flottorp (2010). "Effectiveness of Telemedicine: A Systematic Review of Reviews." *International Journal of Informatics*, 79(11): 736–71.

Feiock, R.C. (2013). "The Institutional Collective Action Framework." *Policy Studies Journal*, 41(3): 397–425.

Feiock, R.C., I.W. Lee, & H.J. Park (2012). "Administrators and Elected Officials' Collaboration Networks: Selecting Partners to Reduce Risk in Economic Development." *Public Administration Review*, 72(s1): 58–68.

Galaskiewicz, J. (1985). "Interorganizational Relations." *Annual Review of Sociology*, 11: 281–304.

Gazley, Beth (2017). "The Current State of Interorganizational Collaboration: Lessons from Human Service Research and Management." *Human Service Organizations: Management, Leadership, and Governance*, 41(1): 1–5.

Gee, E.P. (2000). "Co-opetition: The New Market Milieu." *Journal of Healthcare Management*, 45(6): 359–63.

Goes, J.B. & S.H. Park (1997). "Interorganizational Links and Innovation: The Case of Hospital Service." *Academy of Management Journal*, 40(3): 673–96.

Greve, H.R. (2003). *Organizational Learning from Performance Feedback: A Behavioral Perspective*. Cambridge: Cambridge University Press.

Guo, C. & M. Acar (2005). "Understanding Collaboration among Nonprofit Organizations: Combining Resource Dependency, Institutional, and Network Perspectives." *Nonprofit and Voluntary Sector Quarterly*, 34(3): 340–61.

Hartley, J. 2005. "Innovation in Governance and Public Service: Past and Present." *Public Money and Management*, 25(1): 27–33.

Hartley, Jean & M. Allison (2002). "Good, Better, Best? Inter-Organizational Learning in A Network of Local Authorities." *Public Management Review*, 4 (1): 101–18.

Hartley, J., E. Sorensen, & J. Torfing (2013). "Collaborative Innovation: A Viable Alternative to Market Competition and Organizational Entrepreneurship." *Public Administration Review*, 73(6): 821–30.

Hartman, M., A.B. Martin, J. Benson, & A. Catlin (2020). "National Health Care Spending in 2018: Growth Driven by Accelerations in Medicare and Private Insurance Spending." *Health Affairs*, 39(1), forthcoming.

Herzlinger, R.E. (2006). "Why Innovation in Health Care Is So Hard." *Harvard Business Review*, 84(5): 58–66.

Hicklin, A.K. & E. Godwin (2009). "Agents of Change: The Role of Public Managers in Public Policy." *Policy Studies Journal*, 37(1): 13–20.

Hogg, R. & D. Varda (2016). "Insights into Collaborative Networks of Nonprofit, Private and Public Organizations That Address Complex Health Issues." *Health Affairs*, 35(11): 2014–19.

Holmes, G.M., R.T. Slifkin, R.K. Randolph, & S. Poley (2006). "The Effect of Rural Hospital Closures on Community Economic Health." *Health Service Research*, 41(2): 467–85.

Howlett, M., I. Mukherjee, & J. Koppenjan (2017). "Policy Learning and Policy Networks in Theory and Practice: The Role of Policy Brokers in the Indonesian Biodiesel Policy Network." *Policy and Society*, 36(2): 233–50.

Huang, K. (2014). "Knowledge Sharing in a Third-Party Governed Health and Human Service Network." *Public Administration Review*, 26(4): 593–612.

Hughes, M. & D. Goldenhar (2012). "*Networking a City.*" *Stanford Social Innovation Review*, Summer Issue.

Hughs, D.J., A. Lee, A.W. Tian, A. Newman, & A. Legood (2018). "Leadership, Creativity, and Innovation: A Critical Review and Practical Recommendations." *Leadership Quarterly*, 19(5): 549–69.

Hu, Q., K. Huang, & B. Chen 2019. "Professional Friendship, Resource Competition, and Collaboration in a Homeless Service Delivery Network." *Human Service Organizations: Management, Leadership & Governance*, 44 (2): 110–26.

Hu, Y., F. Wang, I.M. Xierali (2018). "Automated Delineation of Hospital Service Areas and Hospital Referral Regions by Modularity Optimization." *Health Service Research*, 53(1): 236–55.

Ibarra, H. & M. Hunter (2007). "How Leaders Create and Use Networks." *Growth*, 35(1): 101–3.

Isett, K.R., I.A. Mergel, K. LeRoux, P.A. Mischen, & R.K. Rethemeyer. (2011). "Networks in Public Administration Scholarship: Understanding Where We Are and Where We Need to Go." *Journal of Public Administration Research and Theory* 21(suppl.): i157–i173.

Jha, A.K, C.M. DesRoches, E.G. Campbell, K. Donelan, et al. (2009). "Use of Electronic Health Records in U.S. Hospitals." *New England Journal of Medicine*, 360: 1628–38.

Johansen, M.S. & K. LeRoux (2013). "Managerial Networking in Nonprofit Organizations: The Impact of Networking on Organizational and Advocacy Effectiveness." *Public Administration Review*, 73(2): 355–63.

Johansen, M.S. & L. Zhu (2014). "Market Competition, Political Constraint, and Managerial Practice in Public, Nonprofit, and Private American Hospitals." *Journal of Public Administration Research and Theory*, 24(1): 159–84.

Jung, D., A. Wu, & C.W. Chow. (2008). "Towards Understanding the Direct and Indirect Effect of OECs' Transformational Leadership on Firm Innovation." *Leadership Quarterly*, 19(5): 82–594.

Katz, D. & R.L. Kahn. (1978). *The Social Psychology of Organizations.* New York, NY: Wiley.

Keijser, G.M.W.M. & B.L. Kirkman-Liff 1992. "Competitive Bidding for Health Insurance Contracts." *Health Policy*, 21(1): 35–46.

Keehan, S.P., G.A. Cuckler, J.A. Poisal. et al. (2020). "Expected Rebound in Prices Drives Risking Spending Growth." *Health Affairs*, forthcoming.

Kelman, S. (2005). *Unleashing Change: A Study of Organizational Renewal in Government.* Washington, DC: Brookings Institute Press.

Kimberly, J.R. & M.J. Evanisko (1981). "Organizational Innovation: The Influence of Individual, Organizational and Contextual Factors on Hospital Adoption of Technological and Administrative Innovations." *Academy of Management Journal* 24(4): 689–713.

King, G., M. Tomz, & J. Wittenberg (2000). "Making the Most of Statistical Analyses: Improving Interpretation and Presentation." *American Journal of Political Science*, 44(2): 341–55.

Klijn, E.H. (1996). "Analyzing and Managing Policy Processes in Complex Networks." *Administration and Society*, 28(1): 90–119.

Lado, A.A., N.G. Boyd, & S.C. Hanlon (1997). "Competition, Cooperation, and the Search for Economic Rents: A Syncretic Model." *Academy of Management Review*, 22(1): 110–41.

LeTourneau, B. (2004). "Coopetition: An Alternative to Competition." *Journal of Healthcare Management*, 49(2): 81–3.

Levitt, B. & J. G. March (1988). "Organizational Learning." *Annual Review of Sociology*, 14(3): 319–40.

Lewis, J.M., L.M. Ricard, & E.H. Klijin (2018). "How Innovation Drivers, Networking and Leadership Shape Public Sector Innovation." *International Review of Administrative Sciences*, 84(2): 288–307.

Leyden, D.P. & A.N. Link (2015). *Public Sector Entrepreneurship: U.S. Technology and Innovation Policy.* New York, NY: Oxford University Press.

Lieberman, A. (2000). "Networks as Learning Communities." *Journal of Teacher Education*, 51(3): 221–7.

Lynn, M.L. (2005). "Organizational Buffering: Measuring Boundaries and Cores." *Organizational Studies*, 26 (1): 37–61.

Martin, G.P., G. Currie, & R. Finn (2009) "Leadership, Service Reform, and Public Service Networks: The Case of Cancer-Genetics Pilots in the English NHS." *Journal of Public Administration Research and Theory*, 19(4): 769–94.

Maroulis, S. & U. Wilensky (2015). "Social and Task Interdependence in the Street-Level Implementation of Innovation." *Journal of Public Administration Research and Theory*, 25(3): 721–50.

McCarthy, C., P. Ford Carleton, E. Krumpholz, & M.P. Chow (2018). "Accelerating Innovation through Coopetition: The Innovation Learning Network Experience." *Nursing Administration Quarterly*, 42(1): 26–34.

McCrea, A. & L. Zhu (2019). "The Environmental Determinants of Diversity Management: Competition, Collaboration, and Clients." *Public Administration*, 97(4): 942–59.

McKinney, M., A.D. Kaluzny, & H.S. Zuckerman (1991). "Paths and Pacemakers: Innovation Diffusion Networks in Multihospital Systems and Alliances." *Health Care Management Review*, 16(1): 17–23.

Meier, K.J. & Laurence J. O'Toole, Jr. (2001). "Managerial Strategies and Behavior in Networks: A Model with Evidence from U.S. Public Education." *Journal of Public Administration Research and Theory*, 11(3): 271–94.

Meier, K.J. & Laurence J., O'Toole, Jr. (2008). "Management Theory and Occam's Razor: How Public Organizations Buffer the Environment." *Administration and Society*, 39(8): 931–58.

Meier, K.J. &Laurence J. O'Toole, Jr. (2015). "Public Management, Context, and Performance: In the Quest of a More General Theory." *Journal of Public Administration Research and Theory*, 25(1): 237–56.

Meier, K.J., N. Favero, & L. Zhu (2015). "Performance Gaps and Managerial Decisions: A Bayesian Decision Theory of Managerial Action." *Journal of Public Administration Research and Theory*, 25(4): 1221–46.

Mele, V., A. Compagni, & M. Cavazza 2014. "Governing through Evidence: A Study of Technological Innovation in Health Care." *Journal of Public Administration Research and Theory*, 24(4): 843–77.

Mettler, S. (2016). "The Policyscape and the Challenges of Contemporary Politics to Policy Maintenance." *Perspectives on Politics*, 14(2): 369–90.

Milward, H.B. & K. Provan (1998). "Measuring Network Structure." *Public Administration Review*, 76(2): 387–407.

Minstrom, M. & S. Vergari (1998). "Policy Networks and Innovation Diffusion: State Education Reforms." *Journal of Politics*, 60(1): 126–48.

Moczulsak, M., B. Seiler, & J. Stankiewicz (2019). "Coopetition in For-Profit and Nonprofit Organizations—Micro Level." *Management*, 23(2): 138–56.

Moline, J. (1997). "Virtual Reality for Health Care: A Survey." *Studies in Health Technology and Informatics*, 44(1): 3–34.

Moolenaar, N.M., A.J. Daly, & P.J.C. Sleegers (2010). "Occupying the Principal Position: Examining Relationships Between Transformational Leadership, Social Network Position, and Schools' Innovative Climate." *Educational Administration Quarterly*, 46(5): 623–70.

Moore, M. (1995). *Creating Public Value: Strategic Management in Government*. Cambridge, MA: Harvard University Press.

Moynihan, D. & S. Pandey (2008). "The Ties That Bind: Social Networks, Person-Organization Fit, and Turnover Intention." *Journal of Public Administration Research & Theory*, 18(2): 205–27.

Moynihan, D.P., D.P. Carpenter, & G.A. Krause (2012). "Reputation and Public Administration." *Public Administration Review*, 72(1): 26–32.

Muijs, D. & N. Rumyantseva (2014). "Coopetition in Education: Collaborating in A Competitive Environment." *Journal of Educational Change*, 15(1): 1–18.

Negassi, S. & T. Hung (2014). "The Nature of Market Competition and Innovation: Does Competition Drive Innovation Output?" *Economics of Innovation and New Technology*, 23(1): 63–91.

Nembhard, I.M., P. Cherian, & E.H. Bradley (2014), "Deliberate Learning in Health Care: The Effect of Importing Best Practices and Creative Problem Solving on Hospital Performance Improvement." *Medical Care and Research Review*, 71(5): 450–71.

Nicholson-Crotty, S., J. Nicholson-Crotty, & S. Fernandez (2017). "Performance and Management in the Public Sector: Testing a Model of Relative Risk Aversion." *Public Management Review*, 77(4): 603–14.

Nutting, P.A., B.F. Crabtree, W.L. Miller, et al. (2011). "Transforming Physician Practices to Patient-Centered Medical Homes: Lessons from the National Demonstration Project." *Health Affairs*, 30(3): 439–45.

O'Leary, R. & N. Vij (2012). "Collaborative Public Management: Where Have We Been and Where Are We Going?" *American Review of Public Administration*, 42(5): 507–22.

Osborne, S. & K. Brown (2005). *Managing Change and Innovation in Public Service Organizations*. New York, NY: Routledge.

O'Toole, L.J., Jr. (1997). "Treating Networks Seriously: Practical and Research-Based Agendas in Public Administration." *Public Administration Review*, 57(1): 45–52.

Paustian, M.L., J. A. Alexander, D. K. El Reda et al. (2013). "Partial and Incremental PCMH Practice Transformation: Implications for Quality and Costs." *Health Service Research*, 49(1): 52–74.

Peng, T.A. &M. Bourne (2009). "The Coexistence of Competition and Cooperation between Networks: Implications from Two Taiwanese Healthcare Networks." *British Journal of Management*, 20(3): 377–400.

Perednia, D.A. & A. Allen (1995). "Telemedicine Technology and Clinical Applications." JAMA, 273(6): 483–8.

Perry-Smith, J. & P. V. Mannucci 2017. "From Creativity to Innovation: The Social Network Drivers of the Four Phases of the Idea Journey." *Academy of Management Review*, 42(1): 53–79.

Pfeffer, J. & G. Salancik (1978). *The External Control of Organizations: A Resource Dependence Perspective.* New York, NY: Harper & Row.

Powell, W.W. (1990). "Neither Market Nor Hierarchy: Network Forms of Organization." *Research in Organizational Behavior*, 12(2): 295–336.

Powell, W.W. & P.J. DiMaggio (1991). *The New Institutionalism in Organizational Analysis.* Chicago, IL: University of Chicago Press.

Powell, W.W., K.W. Koput, & L. Smith-Doerr (1996). "Interorganizational Collaboration and the Locus of Innovation: Networks of Learning in Biotechnology." *Administrative Science Quarterly*, 41(1): 116–45.

Pressman, J.L. & A. Wildavsky (1984). *Implementation: How Great Expectations in Washington are Dashed in Oakland.* Berkeley and Los Angeles, CA: University of California Press.

Provan, K.G., A. Fish, & J. Sydow (2007). "Interorganizational Networks at the Whole Network Level." *Journal of Management*, 33(3): 479–516.

Provan, K., J.E. Beagles, L. Mercken, & S.J. Leischow (2013). "Awareness of Evidence-Based Practices by Organizations in a Publicly Funded Smoking Cessation Network." *Journal of Public Administration Research and Theory*, 23(1): 133–53.

Raab, J., R. Lemaire, & K.G. Provan (2013). "The Configurational Approach in Organizational Network Research." In *Configurational Theory and Methods in Organizational Research*, P.C. Fiss, B. Cambré, & A. Marx eds. Bingley: Emerald Publishing, pp.225–53.

Ritala, P. &P. Hurmelinna-Laukkanen (2009). What's in it for Me? Creating and Appropriating Value in Innovation-Related Coopetition." *Technovation*, 29 (12): 819–28.

Ritala, P. & L. Sainio (2013). "Coopetition for Radical Innovation: Technology, Market, and Business-Model Perspective." *Technology Analysis & Strategic Management*, 26(2): 155–69.

Ritala, P., A. Golnam, & A. Wegmann (2014). "Coopetition-based Business Models: The Case of Amazon.com." *Industrial Marketing Management*, 43 (2): 236–49.

Robinson, J.C. (2011). "Hospital Market Concentration, Pricing, and Profitability in Orthopedic Surgery and Interventional Cardiology." *American Journal of Managed Care*, 17: e241–8.

Robinson, S. (2006). "A Decade of Treating Networks Seriously." *Policy Studies Journal*, 34(4): 589–98.

Salge, T.O. (2011). "Behavioral Model of Innovation Search: Evidence from Public Hospitals." *Journal of Public Administration Research and Theory*, 21 (1): 181–210.

Schalk, J., R. Torenvlied, & J. Allen (2010). "Network Embeddedness and Public Agency Performance: The Strength of Strong Ties in Dutch Higher Education." *Journal of Public Administration Research and Theory*, 20(3): 629–53.

Smith, S., K. Huang, & S. Peng (2020). "Strategic Orientation and Relationship Building among Dyads in Complex Public Networks: Perspectives from State Asthma Coalitions." *Administration & Society*, forthcoming.

Stentoft, J., O.S. Mikkelsen, & M.B. Ingstrup (2018). "Coopetition Segments in a Public-Sector Context: Insights from a Business Region." *International Journal of Public Administration*, 41(13): 1084–94.

Teece, D. (1992). "Competition, Cooperation, and Innovation: Organizational Arrangements for Regimes of Rapid Technological Progress." *Journal of Economic Behavior & Organization*, 18(1): 1–25.

Tomz, M., J. Wittenberg, & G. King (2003). "CLARIFY: Software for Interpreting and Presenting Statistical Results." *Journal of Statistical Software*, 8(1): 1–30.

Torfing, J. (2019). "Collaborative Innovation in the Public Sector: The Argument." *Public Management Review*, 21(1): 1–11.

Trinh, H.Q., J.W.Begun, and R. Luke (2008). "Hospital Service Duplication: Evidence on the Medical Arms Race." *Health Care Management Review*, 33 (3): 192–202.

Tsai, W. (2002). "Social Structure of 'Coopetition' with a Multiunit Organization: Coordination, Competition, and Inter-Organizational Knowledge Sharing." *Organization Science*, 13(2): 109–222.

Tuckman, H.P. (1998). "Competition, Commercialization, and the Evolution of Nonprofit Organizational Structures." *Journal of Policy Analysis and Management*, 17(2): 175–94.

Uyarra, E., J. Edler, J. Carcia-Estevez, L. Georghiou, & J. Yeow (2014). "Barriers to Innovation through Public Procurement: A Supplier Perspective." *Techovation*, 34(10): 631–45.

Uzzi, B. (1997). "Social Structure and Competition in Interfirm Networks: The Paradox of Embeddedness." *Administrative Science Quarterly*, 42(1): 35–67.

Uzzi, B. & J. Spiro (2005). "Collaboration and Creativity: The Small World Problem." *American Journal of Sociology*, 111(2): 447–504.

van den Broek, J., P. Boselie, & J. Paauwe. (2014). "Multiple Institutional Logics in Health Care." *Public Management Review*, 16(1): 1–20.

van den Broek, J., P. Boselie, & J. Paauwe. (2018). "Cooperative Innovation Through a Talent Management Pool." *European Management Journal*, 36 (1): 135–44.

Varda, Danielle. (2012). "A Systematic Review of Collaboration and Network Research in the Public Affairs Literature: Implications for Public Health Practice and Research."*American Journal of Public Health*, 102(3): 564–71.

Vries, H.D., V. Bekkers, & L. Tummers (2016). "Innovation in the Public Sector: A Systemic Review and Future Research Agenda." *Public Administration*, 94(1): 146–66.

Vries, H.D., V. Bekkers, & L. Tummers (2018). "The Diffusion and Adoption of Public Sector Innovations: A Meta-Synthesis of the Literature." *Perspectives on Public Management and Governance*, 1(3): 159–67.

Walker, R.M. (2008). "An Empirical Evaluation of Innovation Types and Organizational and Environmental Characteristics: Toward a Configuration Framework." *Journal of Public Administration Research and Theory*, 18(4): 591–615.

Walker, R.M. (2014). "Internal and External Antecedents of Process Innovation: A Review and Extension." *Public Management Review*, 16(1): 21–44.

Wang, S. & M.K. Feeney (2014). "Determinants of Information and Communication Technology Adoption in Municipalities." *American Review of Public Administration*, 46 (3): 292–313.

West, D.M. (2004). "E-Government and the Transformation of Service Delivery and Citizen Attitudes." *Public Administration Review*, 64(1): 15–27.

Westra, D., F. Angeli, M. Carree, & D. Ruwaard (2017). "Coopetition in Health Care: A Multi-Level Analysis of Its Individual and Organizational Determinants." *Social Science& Medicine*, 186: 43–51.

Whitford, Andrew. (2007). "Designing Markets: Why Competitive Bidding and Contracting in Government Often Fail to Deliver." *Policy Studies Journal*, 35 (1): 61–85.

Willem, A. & M. Buelens (2007). "Knowledge-Sharing in Public-Sector Organizations: The Effect of Organizational Characteristics." *Journal of Public Administration Research and Theory*, 17(4): 581–606.

Windrum, P. & P. Koch (2008). *Innovation in Public Sector Services: Entrepreneurship, Creativity, and Management*. Northampton, MA: Edward Elgar Publishing Limited.

Yami, S. & A. Nemeh (2014). "Organizational Coopetition for Innovation: The Case for Wireless Telecommunication Sector in Europe." *Industrial Marketing Management*, 43(2): 250–60.

Yu, S.W.Y., C. Hill, M.L. Ricks, J. Bennet, & N.E. Oriol (2017). "The Scope and Impact of Mobile Health Clinics in the United States: A Literature Review." *International Journal of Equity in Health*, 16: 178.

Zhu, L. (2017). "Voices from the Frontline: Network Participation and Local Support for National Policy Reforms." *Journal of Public Administration Research and Theory*, 27(2): 294–300.

Zhu, L. & A. Rutherford (2019). "Managing the Gaps: Shape Managerial Decision Making." *Public Performance& Management Review*, 42(5): 1029–61.

Cambridge Elements ☰

Public and Nonprofit Administration

Andrew Whitford
University of Georgia
Andrew Whitford is Alexander M. Crenshaw Professor of Public Policy in the School of Public and International Affairs at the University of Georgia. His research centers on strategy and innovation in public policy and organization studies.

Robert Christensen
Brigham Young University
Robert Christensen is professor and George Romney Research Fellow in the Marriott School at Brigham Young University. His research focuses on prosocial and antisocial behaviors and attitudes in public and nonprofit organizations.

About the Series
The foundation of this series are cutting-edge contributions on emerging topics and definitive reviews of keystone topics in public and nonprofit administration, especially those that lack longer treatment in textbook or other formats. Among keystone topics of interest for scholars and practitioners of public and nonprofit administration, it covers public management, public budgeting and finance, nonprofit studies, and the interstitial space between the public and nonprofit sectors, along with theoretical and methodological contributions, including quantitative, qualitative and mixed-methods pieces.

The Public Management Research Association
The Public Management Research Association improves public governance by advancing research on public organizations, strengthening links among interdisciplinary scholars, and furthering professional and academic opportunities in public management.

Cambridge Elements ⹀

Public and Nonprofit Administration

Printed in the United States
by Baker & Taylor Publisher Services